鴨 長 明
Kamo no Chōmei

HŌJŌKI

A Buddhist Reflection on Solitude, Imperfection and Transcendence

**Bilingual English and Japanese Texts
with Free Online Audio Recordings**

Translated and Annotated by
Matthew Stavros

With Illustrations by **Reginald Jackson**

TUTTLE Publishing
Tokyo | Rutland, Vermont | Singapore

Table of Contents

About the Translator and Annotator

Matthew Stavros is a historian of Japan at the University of Sydney and the former director of the Kyoto Consortium for Japanese Studies. He is the author of *Kyoto: An Urban History of Japan's Premodern Capital* (University of Hawai'i Press, 2014) and numerous articles on Kyoto's architectural and urban history. His research focuses primarily on the material culture of premodern Japan and eastern Asia, with particular interest in cities, buildings, and religious monuments. He trained in architectural and urban history at Kyoto University and read history at Princeton University where he earned a Ph.D. He teaches modern and classical Japanese language, Japanese history and historiography, and more broadly on the histories and cultures of East and Southeast Asia.

www.mstavros.com | www.kyotohistory.com

Epigraph

No permanence is ours; we are a wave
That flows to fit whatever form it finds

—Hermann Hesse, *The Glass Bead Game*

Introduction

In the thirteenth century, after Japan was rocked by a series of natural and man-made disasters, a wise old man took to the hills in search of inner peace. Living in a small grass hut, isolated from the world, Kamo no Chōmei (1155–1216) put brush to paper and wrote the poetic masterpiece *Hōjōki* about the transcendent power of simplicity and self-reliance. This classic work of Japanese literature is the product of an age of profound social and political turmoil. The classical order, based on the centrality of the emperor and imperial court, was rapidly eroding as provincial warriors vied for control over the levers of state power and wealth. Fierce competition led to protracted wars between military houses, most notably the Taira and Minamoto. The combination of environmental calamity and social instability confirmed for many at the time that the world had entered an age of karmic degeneracy. These "Latter Days of the Dharma" (*mappō*) were characterized by a popular belief that the teachings of the Buddha had become irreparably corrupt. Sentient beings were no longer able to attain enlightenment and social disorder was inevitable. The high and low alike turned for answers to the teachings of Pure Land Buddhism, which held that salvation was attainable through belief in the saving grace of Amida (Sanskrit, Amitābha), the Buddha of immeasurable light. Renunciation was yet another solution. Romanticized images of a life apart, one free from the duty and dross of worldly attachment, inspired a groundswell of literary and artistic production. *Hōjōki* belongs firmly to this time and place, and yet, its message is universal. Today, as many of us negotiate the contradiction of gnawing despondency amidst unprecedented abundance, *Hōjōki* reminds us that clinging to possessions, status, and social recognition can only bring suffering. With unvarnished honesty and profound compassion, this inspirational work invites readers to reassess their attachment to worldly success and to contemplate the inner quiet that comes from solitude.

Kamo no Chōmei was born in Japan's premodern capital of Kyoto to a respected family of hereditary priests attached to the Shimogamo Shrine. He established himself as a formidable poet at a young age, receiving the favor of ranking courtiers and the emperor Gotoba (1180–1239). Despite early success, in 1204, at the age of 49, he was denied a leadership role within the shrine hierarchy. Although it is widely believed that this episode catalyzed Chōmei's sudden decision to take Buddhist vows and begin a life of reclusion, we know from *Hōjōki* that the spate of disasters and political upheavals that rocked the capital three decades earlier had already made him reticent about worldly success. Over the next decade, he moved progressively into smaller and ever more remote houses, finally settling down in a precarious grass hut in the hills southeast of Kyoto. He wrote in *Hōjōki*:

When I had reached the age of sixty,
   —and the dew of life had disappeared—
I built a hut to be my final refuge.

As I get older, my abode gets smaller.

This one's unique:
   It's a *hōjō*, a hut measuring just three meters to a side,
   No more than two meters tall.

The word *hōjō* is an architectural term representing an area of about 32 square feet (three square meters). "*Hōjōki*" literally means "a record of my three-square-meter hut." However, because *hōjō* is often used to signify a monk's quarters, primarily at Zen temples, the word is imbued with religious innuendo. It is not merely small; it is a place of spiritual contemplation and devotion. It was within just such a building that Chōmei determined to live out his remaining years in blissful detachment. Reading *Hōjōki*, one could hardly deny his sincerity:

> To leave this world and reject the cares of the flesh,
> Is to live without bitterness or fear.

By narrating the construction of a simple dwelling, Chōmei deployed a well-worn literary trope in which the house—both architectural and familial—stands as a metaphor for worldly attachment. In Japanese, just as in English, "house" can signify a physical structure or a kinship group, and both are inextricably tied to markers of worldly success. It is a testament to the universality of this notion that the Japanese word for renouncing the world and taking Buddhist vows (*shukke*) literally means "to leave the house." Chōmei plays with this homonym in *Hōjōki*, reminding readers that a fixation upon either defies the universal law of impermanence:

> Great houses fade away,
> Ultimately replaced by lesser ones.

> The same goes for the people who live here.

And...

> A master is to his house,
> What the dew is to the morning glory.
> Which will be the first to fade?

One of the great ironies of *Hōjōki* is that the narrative itself, in its fixation on a tiny hut, reveals Chōmei's irradicable attachment to the world. Indeed, the final third of the work is an extended meditation on the building's location, composition, and contents. In loving detail, Chōmei describes his desk for writing, his altar for praying, a bed made from bracken, books, musical instruments and a small kitchen garden. Even the walls, windows and the rotting leaves in the eaves come in for special mention. This mountain home tethered Chōmei to the world in ways the bonds of family and friendship never did:

> I love my lonely dwelling,
> This simple, one-room hut.

And…

> The Buddha taught non-attachment.

> And yet, the way I love my grass hut,
> That itself is attachment.

Hōjōki can be compared to *Walden* (1854) by Henry David Thoreau. Both works were inspired by deep concern over the negative effects of materialism. Their authors equally fetishized nature and reclusion while conceding an abiding fondness for their dwellings. Tiny houses stand as symbols of their personal philosophies. Chōmei's hut represents the Buddhist ideal of non-attachment while Thoreau's cabin represents the American aspiration to self-reliance. Both works have had a lasting impact on Western and Eastern thought, inspiring generations of readers to reconsider their relationship with material possessions and the natural world.

Hōjōki was modeled closely on a tenth-century memoir entitled *Chiteiki* (*Record of a Pond Pavilion*), written by the bureaucrat and sinophile Yoshishige no Yasutane (c. 933–1002). *Chiteiki* was itself inspired by the writing of the Tang poet-official Bai Juyi (772–846), whose work exemplifies the classical Chinese paradigm of the scholar-official longing for reclusion. Chōmei did not merely echo *Chiteiki*, he almost certainly copied certain passages verbatim, albeit translating them from Sino-Japanese (*kanbun*) into Classical Japanese (*bungo*). *Hōjōki* is considered a masterpiece of Classical Japanese, a literary style that combines Chinese characters (*kanji*) and the Japanese orthography (*kana*) into a lyrical syntax that is accessible and well-suited to Japanese aesthetics. By transposing the tropes of earlier works, Chōmei codified many of the aesthetic qualities that define medieval Japanese literature. *Hōjōki* exemplifies an ethos deeply colored by *mappō* thought and a disconsolate mindfulness about the evanescence of existence. Although the modern reader may be daunted by the gloomy tone, it is important to note that Chōmei and his successors gleefully reveled in the pathos of impermanence (*mujō*), finding beauty in the fleeting and ephemeral. In doing so, they contributed to an indigenous aesthetic that celebrated concepts like *wabi* (subdued simplicity), *sabi* (rustic elegance), and *mono no aware* (an empathy toward things). In concert with Zen paradigms about simplicity and asceticism, these ideas inspired much of the writing that emerged over the following four centuries. Key examples include Saigyō's (1118–1190) *Sankashū* (*Poems of a Mountain*

Home) and Yoshida Kenkō's (c. 1283–c. 1352) *Tsurezuregusa* (*Essays in Idleness*). The same ethos of detachment is found in Matsuo Bashō's (1644–1694) *Oku no hosomichi* (*Narrow Road to the Deep North*).

Hōjōki is an archetypal example of a mode of writing called *zuihitsu*, literally "following the brush." Characterized by loosely connected personal observations about the author's surroundings, *zuihitsu* texts flit from one theme to another without regard for an overarching narrative. They are peppered with deeply subjective, sometimes acerbic, comments about people, places and ideas. Despite having an air of privacy and informality, they were clearly written for public consumption. For as long as Japanese literature has been read in English, commentators have struggled to characterize *zuihitsu* as a genre, frequently calling it "stream-of-consciousness" literature. Paradoxically, modern technology has provided a very close approximation in the form of the blog, with its short, disjointed passages, often composed in a chatting tone, rife with judgment. The eleventh-century *Makura no sōshi* (*Pillow Book of Sei Shōnagon*) (c. 1000) is the earliest major work of *zuihitsu*. It may have inspired Chōmei, but the aesthetics of *Hōjōki* belong unmistakably to the medieval era (13th to 16th c.). Kenkō's *Tsurezuregusa* is widely believed to have been modeled on *Hōjōki*.

Unfortunately, the original text of *Hōjōki* is lost to history. The oldest known manuscript, which is owned by the temple of Daifukukōji in Kyoto Prefecture, dates to about 1244. Down the centuries, the text has been copied and recopied countless times, recited on stages and street corners, parodied, and set to music. As a result, there are now numerous versions, none of which can claim to be authoritative. The text that appears in this book was published by Meibun-sha in 1906 and is now in the public domain. It was one of the earliest mass-produced publications of *Hōjōki* and it appeared just as the work was being integrated into school curricula across Japan, where it remains firmly entrenched to this day.

This book represents the first unabridged parallel English translation of *Hōjōki*. For general readers, the juxtaposition of the Classical Japanese and the English verse stands as a constant reminder of the work's provenance, rooted firmly in the history and culture of medieval Japan. For students of the language and researchers, it enables critical engagement with the text, inviting them to grapple with the interpretations provided and, perhaps, attempt their own. Romanization is provided as a reading aid with one important caveat: there remains some ambiguity about how certain words and phrases in Classical Japanese are read aloud in different contexts. Although the romanization provided here can be considered conventional, it is important to note that other readings are also possible. Indeed, the question of how precisely to read premodern texts such as this one animates an entire academic field. This book also includes scholarly notes and maps that shed light on *Hōjōki's* cultural and contextual details, literary allusions, and the ways Chōmei was influenced by earlier writings. Original illustrations by Reginald Jackson add visual impact to this moving narrative on solitude and transcendence.

Translator's Note and Acknowledgements

Hōjōki has long been special to me. It was among the first works of early Japanese literature I read and the very first Classical Japanese text I studied. It fostered an affection for Kyoto and medieval aesthetics that shaped my life and career. I revisit its pages often and always find new inspiration.

When I began work on this translation, the world was plagued by a menacing crisis. A novel coronavirus had swept the globe, claiming countless lives, sickening millions, and devastating economies. It was the outbreak of COVID-19 that drew me back to *Hōjōki* and motivated me to prepare this book. I hope its message will help readers maintain perspective even during challenging times and remember that, as Chōmei himself writes, "the flow of the river never ceases." This too shall pass.

I owe a debt of gratitude to the many students with whom I have read *Hōjōki* over the years. Their novel interpretations never failed to inspire new ways of thinking about Chōmei's style. It was they who convinced me that the work is best rendered in the fashion of a long-form poem, as it appears in this book. I feel this format captures well the economy of words and poetic lyricism of the original. It also lends itself to a more deliberate reading style, one that embraces pregnant pauses and the momentary flights of imagination they inspire. Although the original text does not have discrete parts, I have divided this book into fourteen separate chapters and assigned to each a title of my own invention. Doing so, I believe, helps highlight Chōmei's spiritual journey, moving first from bitter disillusionment to detachment, ultimately arriving at transcendence.

It gave me great joy to watch Reggie Jackson draft the illustrations for this book. He brought to the task a keen understanding of *Hōjōki* and sublime artistic ability. To find these two qualities in one person, and much more besides, is rare and special. This book is enhanced immeasurably by his contribution. Although I have long aspired to the title, I suppose it is time for me to concede that Reggie truly is Ludi Magister. Thanks is also due to Robert Goforth and Winifred Bird at Tuttle for their wise counsel and professionalism. For being constant sources of solace in this turbulent world, I record my eternal gratitude to Kyoko, Miyako, and Kent.

This book is dedicated to my sister, Rosemarie Roberts. My life has been enriched in countless ways by Rose's strength of character, good will and reliable friendship. She embodies one of *Hōjōki's* most important messages about hope.

Matthew Stavros
Sydney

Hōjōki

Prologue

The flow of the river never ceases,
And the water never stays the same.

Bubbles float on the surface of pools,
Bursting, re-forming, never lingering.

They're like the people in this world and their dwellings.

冒頭

行く川のながれは絶えずして、
しかももとの水にあらず。
よどみに浮ぶうたかたは、
かつ消えかつ結びて久しく
とゞまることなし。
世の中にある人とすみかと、
またかくの如し

Bōtō

Yuku kawa no nagare wa taezu shite,
shikamo moto no mizu ni arazu.

Yodomi ni ukabu utakata wa,
katsu kie katsu musubite hisashiku
todomaru koto nashi.

Yo no naka ni aru hito to sumika to,
mata kaku no gotoshi.

In our bejeweled capital:
    Fine buildings stand in rows,
    Their gables competing for preeminence.[1]

The homes of the elite:
    One might think they're eternal,
    But ask around and you'll find,
    Those with a long history are rare indeed.

Collapsing this year, they are rebuilt the next,
Ultimately, great houses fade away,
Replaced by lesser ones.

The same goes for the people who live here.

玉しきの都の中にむねをならべ、
いらかをあらそへる、
たかきいやしき
人のすまひは、
代々を經て盡きせぬもの
なれど、これをまことかと尋ぬれば、
昔ありし家はまれなり。

或はこぞ破れてことしは造り、
あるは大家ほろびて小家となる。

住む人もこれにおなじ。

Tamashiki no miyako no naka ni mune o narabe,
iraka o arasoeru,
takaki iyashiki
hito no sumai wa,
daidai o hete tsukisenu mono
naredo, kore o makoto ka to tazunureba,
mukashi arishi ie wa mare nari.

Aru wa kozo yaburete kotoshi wa tsukuri,
Aru wa taika horobite shōka to naru.

Sumu hito mo kore ni onaji.

This place and its crowds seem eternal, unchanging,
And yet, of the twenty or thirty people I knew long ago,
Only one or two are still around.

Just as people die in the evening and others are born the
next morning:
    So are we like the bubbles on water.

Nameless, one dies as another is born,
From whence do they come,
And to where do they go?

And all these anonymous, temporary abodes!
For whom do we bother?
Why try so hard only to delight the senses?

所も変らず、人も多かれど、
いにしへ見し人は、
二三十人が中に、わづかに
ひとりふたりなり

あしたに死し、
ゆふべに生る、ならひ、
たゞ水の泡にぞ似たりける。

知らず、生れ死ぬる人、
いづかたより來りて、
いづかたへか去る。

又知らず、かりのやどり、
誰が為に心を悩まし、
何によりてか目をよろこばしむる。

Tokoro mo kawarazu, hito mo ōkaredo,
inishie mishi hito wa,
ni-sanjū nin ga naka ni, wazuka ni
hitori futari nari.

Ashita ni shishi,
yūbe ni naruru narai,
tada mizu no awa ni zo nitarikeru.

Shirazu, umare shinuru hito,
izukata yori kitarite,
izukata e ka saru.

Mata shirazu, kari no yadori,
dare ga tame ni kokoro o nayamashi,
nani ni yorite ka me o yorokobashimuru.

A master is to his house,
What the dew is to the morning glory.
Which will be the first to fade?

Sometimes the dew evaporates,
While the flower remains.

But the flower will surely wilt,
Under the rays of the morning sun.

And yet, sometimes, the dew remains,
Clinging to a shriveled petal.

No matter:
The dew will surely vanish by evening.

そのあるじとすみかと、
無常をあらそひ去るさま、
いはゞ朝顔の露にことならず。

或は露おちて花のこれり。

のこるといへども朝日に枯れぬ。

或は花はしぼみて、露なほ消えず。

消えずといへども、ゆふべを
待つことなし。

Sono aruji to sumika to,
mujō o arasoi saru sama,
iwaba asagao no tsuyu ni koto narazu.

Aru wa tsuyu ochite hana nokoreri.

Nokoru to iedomo asahi ni karenu.

Aru wa hana wa shibomite, tsuyu nao kiezu.

Kiezu to iedomo, yūbe o
matsu koto nashi.

Suffering

1
The Fire of the Angen Era

Over forty springs and autumns,
　　—Ever since I came to understand the essence of
　　being—
I've witnessed many awful things.

One night, long ago,
There was a tremendous wind.
　　—It would have been the twenty-eighth day of the
　　fourth month, during the third year of Angen*—

At about eight o'clock in the evening,
Fire broke out in the capital's southeast and spread to the
northwest.

It finally reached the Suzaku Gate of the Imperial Palace,
the Great Hall of State, the Imperial University, and the
Ministry of the Interior:
　　All were reduced to ash in a single night.

---

*1177

安元の大火

およそ物の心を知れりしよりこのかた、
四十あまりの春秋をおくれる間に
世のふしぎを見ることや、
たびたびになりぬ。

いにし安元三年四月廿八日かとよ、
風烈しく吹きて、しづかならざりし夜、
戌の時ばかり、
都のたつみより火
出で來りていぬゐに至る。

はてには朱雀門、大極殿、大學寮、
民部の省まで移りて、
ひとよがほどに、塵灰となりにき。

Angen no taika

Oyoso mono no kokoro o shirerishi yori kono kata,
shijū amari no shunjū o okureru aida ni
yo no fushigi o miru koto yaya
tabitabi ni narinu.

Inishi Angen san-nen shi-gatsu nijūhachi-nichi ka to yo,
kaze hageshiku fukite, shizuka narazarishi yoru,
inu no koku bakari,
miyako no tatsumi yori hi
idekitarite inui ni itaru.

Hateni wa Suzakumon, Daigokuden, Daigakuryō,
Minbu no shō made utsurite,
hitoyo ga hodo ni, jinkai to nari ni ki.

The Fire of the Angen Era (1177), by Reginald Jackson.

The fire is thought to have started at a lodge for invalids,
Near the intersection of Higuchi and Tominokōji roads.

The wind blew wildly,
This way and that,
Feeding the flames, which spread out like a fan.

Houses in the distance were engulfed in smoke.
The ground nearby, bathed in frightful flames.

The sky was filled with cinders,
Glowing crimson, it reflected the fires below.

火本は樋口富の小路とかや、
病人を宿せるかりやより出で來けるとなむ。

吹きまよふ風にとかく移り行くほどに、
扇をひろげたるが如くすゑひろになりぬ。

遠き家は煙にむせび、
近きあたりはひたすらほのほを
地に吹きつけたり。

空には灰を吹きたてたれば、
火の光に映じてあまねくくれなゐなる中に、
風に堪へず。

Hi no moto wa Higuchi–Tominokōji to ka ya,
byōnin o yadoseru kariya yori idekikeru to namu.

Fukimayou kaze ni tokaku utsuriyuku hodo ni,
ōgi o hirogetaru ga gotoku suehiro ni narinu.

Tōki ie wa kemuri ni musebi,
chikaki atari wa hitasura honō o
chi ni fukitsuketari.

Sora ni wa hai o fukitatetareba,
hi no hikari ni eijite amaneku kurenai naru naka ni,
kaze ni taezu.

Driven by slashing winds,
Flames leapt across city blocks as if taking flight.

Those caught in the midst of it,
Whatever could they have felt?

Overcome by smoke,
Some fell to the ground.

Others were swallowed by flames,
Perishing immediately.

Most couldn't save themselves,
Let alone protect their possessions.

So much lost:
All the treasures of this world, turned to ash.

吹き切られたるほのほ、
飛ぶが如くにして一二町を越えつゝ
移り行く。

その中の人うつゝ心ならむや。

あるひは煙にむせびてたふれ伏し、
或は炎にまぐれてたちまちに死しぬ。

或は又わづかに身一つからくして
遁れたれども、
資材を取り出づるに及ばず。

七珍萬寶、さながら灰塵となりにき。

そのつひえいくそばくぞ。

Fukikiraretaru honō,
tobu ga gotoku ni shite ichi-ni chō o koetsutsu
utsuriyuku.

Sono naka no hito utsutsu kokoro naramuya.

Arui wa kemuri ni musebite taorefushi,
aru wa honō ni magurete tachimachi ni shishinu.

Aru wa mata wazuka ni mi hitotsu karaku shite
nogaretaredomo,
shizai o toriizuru ni oyobazu.

Shicchin manpō, sanagara kaijin to nariniki.

Sono tsuie ikusobaku zo.

The homes of sixteen noblemen and countless others were burned.

It amounted to a third of the capital.

Several thousand men and women died,
Countless horses and cattle perished.

Everything we do in this life is senseless,
But wasting one's wealth on the building of a house in this perilous capital is especially foolish.

このたび公卿の家十六燒けたり。

ましてその外は數を知らず。

すべて都のうち、
三分が一に及べりとぞ。

男女死ぬるもの數千人、
馬牛のたぐひ邊際を知らず。

人のいとなみみなおろかなる中に、
さしも危き京中の家を作るとて
寶をつひやし心をなやますことは、
すぐれたあぢきなくぞ侍るべき。

Konotabi kugyō no ie jūroku yaketari.

Mashite sono hoka wa kazu o shirazu.

Subete miyako no uchi,
sanbun ga ichi ni oyoberi to zo.

Danjo shinuru mono sūsen'nin,
bagyū no tagui hensai o shirazu.

Hito no itonami mina oroka naru naka ni,
sashimo abunaki kyōchū no ie o tsukuru to te
takara o tsuiyashi kokoro o nayamasu koto wa,
sugureta ajiki naku zo haberubeki.

Historical sources such as Gyokuyō confirm there was another fire later that year that devastated the city's southern sections. The Japanese capital (today called Kyoto) was established in 794 by Emperor Kanmu and planned according to a grid-like urban model imported from China. The imperial palace was enclosed within an exclusive compound located at the top and center of the city. The rest of the urban landscape was composed of square blocks measuring 394 feet (120 meters) to a side. The great Suzaku Road, measuring 269 feet (82 meters) wide, extended south from the palace and divided the city into symmetrical halves. A weakening of government institutions and several topographical factors conspired to prevent the classical urban plan from being fully realized. The western half, for example, failed to thrive and, by the twelfth century, had largely reverted to farmland or scrub.

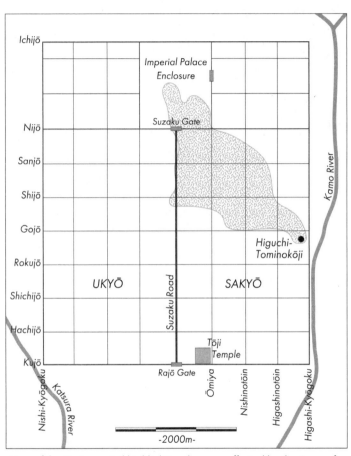

Map of the Kyoto capital highlighting the area affected by the Angen fire of 1177.

2
The Whirlwind of the Jishō Era

It was the fourth year of the Jishō era,*
On about the twenty-ninth day of the fourth month,
A great whirlwind appeared near the intersection of Naka-
mikado and Kyōgoku roads.

It ripped through the city,
Down to the Rokujō area.

It relentlessly lashed three or four city blocks,
Leaving no houses, big or small, unscathed.

Some houses were completely razed,
Others were left with their bare frames exposed.

---

*1180

治承の旋風

また治承四年卯月廿九日のころ、
中の御門京極のほどより、
大なるつじかぜ起りて、
六條わたりまで、
いかめしく吹きけること　侍りき。

三四町をかけて吹きまくるに、
その中にこもれる家ども、
大なるもちひさきも、
一つとしてやぶれざるはなし。

さながらひらにたふれたるもあり。

けたはしらばかり殘れるもあり。

Jishō no tsujikaze

Mata Jishō yo-nen Uzuki nijūku-nichi no koro,
Nakanomikado–Kyōgoku no hodo yori,
ōinaru tsujikaze okorite,
Rokujō watari made,
ikameshiku fukikeru koto haberiki.

San-shi chō o kakete fukimakuru ni,
sono naka ni komoreru iedomo,
dai naru mo chiisaki mo,
hitotsu to shite yaburezaru wa nashi.

Sanagara hira ni taoretaru mo ari.

Keta hashira bakari nokoreru mo ari.

The gale ripped off the tops of gates,
Depositing the debris four or five blocks away.

It toppled the walls between lots,
Merging one property with the next.

Countless household treasures were flung into the sky.

Thatch and timber roofing,
Danced wildly like dry leaves in the winter.

Dust rose up like smoke,
Occluding everything from sight.

The din of the whirlwind was so loud,
Every voice was drowned out.

又門の上を吹き放ちて、
四五町がほかに置き、
又垣を吹き拂ひて隣と
一つになせり。

いはむや家の内のたから、
數をつくして空にあがり、
ひはだぶき板のたぐひ、
冬の木の葉の風に亂る、がごとし。

塵を煙のごとく吹き立てたれば、
すべて目も見えず。

おびたゞしくなりとよむ音に、
物いふ聲も聞えず。

Mata mon no ue o fukihanachite,
shi-go chō ga hoka ni oki,
mata kaki o fukiharaite tonari to
hitotsu ni naseri.

Iwamuya ie no uchi no takara,
kazu o tsukushite sora ni agari,
hiwadabuki ita no tagui,
fuyu no konoha no kaze ni midaruru ga gotoshi.

Chiri o kemuri no gotoku fuki tatetareba,
subete me mo miezu.

Obitadashiku nari toyomu oto ni,
mono iu koe mo kikoezu.

I recall it being like the winds of hell.

Houses were not the only things destroyed.

Countless people lost their lives in the scramble to save their homes.

I heard even more cries of anguish,
When the wind turned southwest.

Although whirlwinds are not uncommon,
Has there ever been one so powerful?

かの地獄の業風なりとも、
かばかりにとぞ覺ゆる。

家の損亡するのみならず、
これをとり繕ふ間に、
身をそこなひて、
かたはづけるもの數を知らず。

この風ひつじさるのかたに移り行きて、
多くの人のなげきをなせり。

つじかぜはつねに吹くものなれど、
かゝることやはある。

Kano jigoku no gōfū nari tomo,
kabakari ni to zo oboyuru.

Ie no sonmō suru nomi narazu,
kore o tori tsukurou aida ni,
mi o sokonaite,
katawazukeru mono kazu o shirazu.

Kono kaze hitsuji saru no kata ni utsuriyukite,
ōku no hito no nageki o naseri.

Tsujikaze wa tsune ni fuku mono naredo,
kakaru koto ya wa aru.

It wasn't typical.

I can't help thinking it was a bad omen.

たゞごとにあらず。

さるべき物のさとしかなとぞ疑ひ侍りし。

Tadagoto ni arazu.

Sarubeki mono no satoshi kana to zo utagai haberishi.

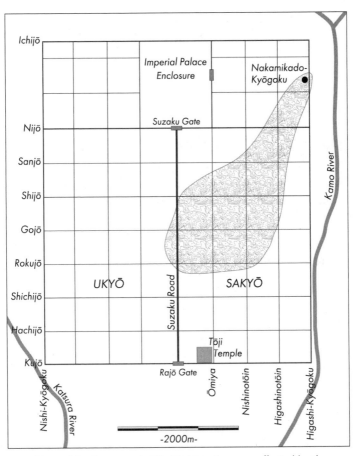

Map of the Kyoto capital highlighting the area affected by the
whirlwind of the Jishō era in 1180.

3
The Relocation of the Capital

In the sixth month of the same year,*
The capital was suddenly moved![2]

Utterly unexpected!

It's said that the capital was established during the reign of
Emperor Saga,
Some four hundred years ago.[3]

Moving the capital is no small matter,
And should never be done on a whim.

It was all so very sudden,
Everyone was bewildered and apprehensive.

---

*1180

福原の遷都

又おなじ年の六月の頃、
にはかに都うつり侍りき。

いと思ひの外なりし事なり。

大かたこの京のはじめを聞けば、
嵯峨の天皇の御時、
都とさだまりにけるより後、
既に數百歳を經たり。

異なるゆゑなくて、
たやすく改まるべくもあらねば、
これを世の人、たやすからずうれへ
あへるさま、ことわりにも過ぎたり。

Fukuhara no sento

Mata onaji toshi no rokugatsu no koro,
niwakani miyako utsuri haberiki.

Ito omoi no hoka narishi koto nari.

Ōkata kono miyako no hajime o kikeba,
Saga no tennō no ontoki,
miyako to sadamari ni keru yori nochi,
Sude ni sū-hyaku-sai wo hetari.

Kotonaru yue nakute,
tayasuku aratamaru beku mo araneba,
kore o yo no hito, tayasukarazu uree
aeru sama, kotowari ni mo sugitari.

Ultimately, once his Majesty relocated to the new capital
at Nanba in the province of Settsu,
Ministers and the high nobility soon followed suit.

How could anyone who served the court stay behind?

Those who crave status,
And those who depend on the patronage of a master:
    They were the first to go.

Those who missed their chance,
And those who failed to gain office or lost their way:
    They were left lamenting.

されどとかくいふかひなくて、
みかどよりはじめ奉りて、
大臣公卿ことごとく
攝津國難波の京にうつり給ひぬ。

世に仕ふるほどの人、
誰かひとりふるさとに殘り居らむ。

官位に思ひをかけ、主君のかげを
頼むほどの人は、一日なりとも、
とくうつらむとはげみあへり。

時を失ひ世にあまされて、
ごする所なきものは、
愁へながらとまり居れり。

Saredo tokaku iu kainakute,
mikado yori hajime tatematsurite,
daijin kugyō kotogotoku
Settsu no kuni Nanba no miyako ni utsuri tamainu.

Yo ni tsukauru hodo no hito,
dareka hitori furusato ni nokori iramu.

Kan'i ni omoi o kake, shukun no kage o
tanomu hodo no hito wa, ichi-nichi nari tomo,
toku utsuramu to hagemi aeri.

Toki o ushinai yo ni amasarete,
gosuru tokoro naki mono wa,
ureenagara tomari ireri.

The homes of those who had vied for influence,
Daily fell into disrepair.

Some were dismantled,
Their timber floated down the Yodo River.[4]

The land where they had stood,
Turned to fields before our eyes.

People's values also changed.

They came to prefer horse and saddle,
No need for ox-driven carriages.[5]

Everyone sought land along the southwestern seaboard,
No interests in the estates of the northeastern provinces.[6]

Around that time,
I had occasion to visit the new capital at Settsu.

軒を争ひし人のすまひ、
日を經つゝあれ行く。

家はこぼたれて淀川に浮び、
地は目の前に畠となる。

人の心皆あらたまりて、
たゞ馬鞍をのみ重くす。

牛車を用とする人なし。

西南海の所領をのみ願ひ、
東北國の庄園をば好まず。

その時、おのづから事のたより
ありて、津の國今の京に到れり。

Noki o arasoishi hito no sumai,
hi o tatsutsu areyuku.

Ie wa kobotarete Yodogawa ni ukabi,
chi wa me no mae ni hatake to naru.

Hito no kokoro mina aratamarite,
tada uma-kura o nomi omokusu.

Gissha o yō to suru hito nashi.

Seinankai no shoryō o nomi negai,
Tōhoku no kuni no shōen o ba konomazu.

Sono toki, onozukara koto no tayori
arite, Tsu no kuni ima no miyako ni itareri.

I could see that it was terribly cramped,
No space to lay out a proper urban grid.

In the north, the land rose high into the hills,
In the south, it sloped down to the sea.

The sound of crashing waves was constant,
Sea gusts were particularly violent.

Located deep in the mountains,
The imperial palace was reminiscent of the Maro Palace,
Bearing all the rustic elegance the name implies.[7]

所のありさまを見るに、
その地ほどせまくて、
條理をわるにたらず。

北は山にそひて高く、
南は海に近くてくだれり。

なみの音つねにかまびすしくて、
潮風殊にはげしく、
内裏は山の中なれば、
かの木の丸殿もかくやと、
なかなかやうかはりて、
いうなるかたも侍りき。

Tokoro no arisama o miru ni,
sono chi hodo semakute,
jōri o waru ni tarazu.

Kita wa yama ni soite takaku,
minami wa umi ni chikakute kudareri.

Nami no oto tsune ni kamabisushikute,
shiokaze koto ni hageshiku,
dairi wa yama no naka nareba,
kano Ki no Maro-dono mo kaku ya to,
nakanaka yōkawarite,
iu naru kata mo haberiki.

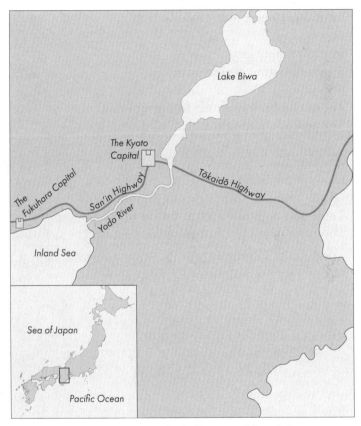

Map of central Japan showing the location of the Fukuhara capital along the Inland Sea.

Day after day, houses were dismantled.

With their timber clogging up the river,
I wondered where they would be rebuilt.

So many empty lots,
So few new structures going up.

The old capital was already falling into ruin,
The new one, yet to rise.

Like clouds,
Everyone felt adrift.

Those who originally lived at the site of the new capital,
They were distraught for having lost their land.

日々にこぼちて川もせきあへず
はこびくだす家は、
いづくにつくれるにかあらむ。

なほむなしき地は多く、
作れる屋はすくなし。

ふるさとは既にあれて、
新都はいまだならず。

ありとしある人、
みな浮雲のおもひをなせり。

元より此處に居れるものは、
地を失ひてうれへ、

Hibi ni kobochite kawa mo sekiaezu
hakobikudasu ie wa,
izuku ni tsukureru ni ka aramu.

Nao munashiki chi wa ōku,
tsukureru oku wa sukunashi.

Furusato wa sude ni arete,
shinto wa imada narazu.

Aritoshi aru hito,
mina ukigumo no omoi o naseri.

Moto yori koko ni ireru mono wa,
chi o ushinaite uree,

Those who moved in,
They were exasperated by the task of rebuilding.

The people one might expect to see riding carriages,
Up and down the avenues,
They had all taken to horseback.

Those who formerly wore fine court robes,
Had donned common dress.

Capital culture itself began to change,
As former gentlemen became rustic soldiers.

The changes were bemoaned as harbingers of chaos,
And sure enough, as time passed, anguish and confusion
reigned.[8]

今うつり住む人は、
土木のわづらひあることをなげく。

道のほとりを見れば、
車に乗るべきはうまに乗り、
衣冠布衣なるべきはひたゝれを着たり。

都のてふりたちまちにあらたまりて、
唯ひなびたる武士にことならず。

これは世の亂る、瑞相とか
聞きおけるもしるく、
日を經つゝ世の中うき立ちて、
人の心も治らず、

ima utsurisumu hito wa,
doboku no wazurai aru koto o nageku.

Michi no hotori o mireba,
kuruma ni norubeki wa uma ni nori,
ikan-hoi narubeki wa hitatare o kitari.

Miyako no tefuri tachimachi ni aratamarite,
tada hinabitaru bushi ni kotonarazu.

Kore wa yo no midaruru zuisō toka
kikiokeru mo shiruku,
hi o tatsutsu yo no naka ukitachite,
hito no kokoro mo naorazu,

Indeed, cries of outrage eventually grew so loud,
The capital was moved back to its original location that
very same winter.

But what about all those dismantled houses?
They could not be easily rebuilt.

It's said that the nation, long ago,
Was governed with compassion by wise rulers.

The Imperial Palace was covered with common thatch,
And the eaves were left ragged.

民のうれへつひにむなしからざりければ、
おなじ年の冬、猶この京に歸り給ひにき。

されどこぼちわたせりし家どもは
いかになりにけるにか、
ことごとく元のやうにしも作らず。

ほのかに傳へ聞くに、
いにしへのかしこき御代には、
あはれみをもて國ををさめ給ふ。

則ち御殿に茅をふきて軒をだにとゝのへず。

tami no uree tsui ni munashikarazarikereba,
onaji toshi no fuyu, nao kono miyako ni kaeritamai ni ki.

Saredo kobochiwataseri shi iedomo wa
ika ni nari ni keru ni ka,
kotogotoku moto no yōni shimo tsukurazu.

Honoka ni tsutae kiku ni,
inishie no kashikoki ondai ni wa,
awaremi o mote kuni o osametamau.

Sunawachi goten ni kaya o fukite noki o dani totonoezu.

4

The Famine of the Yōwa Era

Later, there was a famine that lasted two years and brought immeasurable misery.

I think it was during the Yōwa era,*
So long ago I've forgotten.[9]

In spring and summer,
The sun was fierce.

In autumn and winter,
Typhoons and floods.

Terrible calamities followed, one after another,
Until all the grain crops failed.

People plowed in spring and planted in summer,
All to no avail.

The merriment that comes with an autumn harvest was lost,
Stocking up for winter became impossible.

---

*1181–1182

養和の飢饉

又養和のころかとよ、久しくなりてたしかにも覺えず、二年が間、世の中飢渇して、あさましきこと侍りき。

或は春夏日でり、或は秋冬大風、大水などよからぬ事どもうちつゞきて、五穀ことごとくみのらず。

むなしく春耕し、夏植うるいとなみありて、秋かり冬收むるぞめきはなし。

Yōwa no kikin

Mata Yōwa no koro ka to yo,
hisashiku narite tashika ni mo oboezu,
ni-nen ga aida, yo no naka kikatsu shite,
asamashiki koto haberiki.

Aru wa haru natsu hideri, aru wa aki fuyu taifū,
ōmizu nado yokaranu koto domo uchitsuzukite,
gokoku kotogotoku minorazu.

Munashiku haru tagayashi,
natsu uuru itonami arite,
aki kari fuyu osamuru zo meki wa nashi.

Throughout the provinces,
People left their farms and homes.

Some took to the hills.

Various prayers were chanted,
Many rituals performed,
All to no avail.

The capital has always relied on the hinterland,
So when supplies stopped flowing in,
All dignity was lost.

Having given up hope,
People were resigned to offloading all their possessions.

I saw not a single exception.

これによりて、國々の民、或は地を捨てて堺を出で、或は家をわすれて山にすむ。

さまざまの御祈はじまりて、なべてならぬ法ども行はるれど、さらにそのしるしなし。

京のならひなに事につけても、みなもとは田舎をこそたのめるに、絶えてのぼるものなければ、さのみやはみさをも作りあへむ。

念じわびつゝ、さまざまの寶もの、かたはしより捨つるがごとくすれども、さらに目みたつる人もなし。

Kore ni yorite, kuniguni no tami,
aru wa chi o sutete sakai o ide,
aru wa ie o wasurete yama ni sumu.

Samazama no oinori hajimarite,
nabete naranu nori domo okonawaruredo,
sara ni sono shirushi nashi.

Miyako no narai nanigoto ni tsukete mo,
minamoto wa inaka o kosotanomeru ni,
taete noboru mono nakereba,
sanomiya wa misao mo tsukuriaemu.

Nenji wabitsutsu, samazama no takaramono,
katawashi yori sutetsuru ga gotoku suredomo,
sara ni me mitatsuru hito mo nashi.

In the little trade that remained,
Grain had become more valuable than gold.

Beggars lined the streets,
The sounds of their suffering filled my ears.

The year ended in this pathetic way.

Everyone hoped the new year would bring renewal,
But things only got worse when plague struck.

As time passed and everyone died of starvation,
We began feeling like fish trapped in a shrinking pool.

たまたま易ふるものは、
金をかろくし、粟を重くす。

乞食道の邊におほく、
うれへ悲しむ聲耳にみてり。

さきの年かくの如くからくして暮れぬ。

明くる年は立ちなほるべきかと思ふに、
あまさへえやみうちそひて、
まさるやうにあとかたなし。

世の人みな飢ゑ死にければ、
日を經つゝきはまり行くさま、
少水の魚のたとへに叶へり。

Tamatama kauru mono wa,
kane o karokushi, awa o omokusu.

Kojiki michi no hotori ni ōku,
uree kanashimu koe mimi ni miteri.

Saki no toshi kaku no gotoku karaku shite kurenu.

Akuru toshi wa tachinaorubeki ka to omou ni,
ama sae eyami uchisoite,
masaru yō ni atokata nashi.

Yo no hito mina ueshinikereba,
hi o tatsutsu kiwamariyuku sama,
shōsui no sakana no tatoe ni kanaeri.

Donning hats and gaiters,
Finely dressed ladies and gentlemen,
Went from house to house, begging frantically.

Right before my eyes,
I saw stricken people suddenly collapse.

Starved bodies lay strewn about the streets,
Slumped and rigid against the walls of houses.

Because they weren't removed,
A dreadful stench arose.

To look upon those rotting corpses,
Was more than one could bear.

はてには笠うちき、
足ひきつゝみ、
よろしき姿したるもの、
ひたすらに家ごとに乞ひありく。

かくわびしれたるものども
ありくかと
見れば則ち斃れふしぬ。

ついひぢのつら、
路頭に飢ゑ死ぬるたぐひは
數もしらず。

取り捨つるわざもなければ、
くさき香世界にみちみちて、
かはり行くかたちありさま、
目もあてられぬこと多かり。

Hate ni wa kasa uchiki,
ashi hikitsutsumi,
yoroshiki sugata shitaru mono,
hitasura ni ie goto ni koi ariku.

Kaku wabishiretaru mono domo
ariku ka to
mireba sunawachi taore fushinu.

Tsuiiji no tsura,
rotō ni ueshinuru tagui wa
kazu mo shirazu.

Tori sutsuru waza mo nakereba,
kusaki kaori sekai ni michimichite,
kawari yuku katachi arisama,
me mo aterarenu koto ōkari.

The river's edge was choked with bodies,
Not room enough for horses or carts to pass.[10]

With laborers and woodsmen exhausted,
Even firewood disappeared.

Without another possession in the world,
Some people tore down their houses and took the timber
to market.

But alas, I heard that the value wasn't enough to live on for
even a day.

I was baffled to see firewood with crimson paint, flecked
with silver and gold.

いはむや河原などには、
馬車の行きちがふ道だにもなし。

しづ、山がつも、力つきて、
薪にさへともしくなりゆけば、
たのむかたなき人は、
みづから家をこぼちて
市に出で、これを賣るに、
一人がもち出でたるあたひ、
猶一日が命をさゝふるにだに
及ばずとぞ。

あやしき事は、
かゝる薪の中に、につき、
しろがねこがねのはくなど
所々につきて
見ゆる木のわれあひまじれり。

Iwamuya kawara nado ni wa,
basha no yukichigau michi dani mo nashi.

Shizu, yama ga tsumo, chikara tsukite,
maki ni sae tomoshiku nariyukeba,
tanomu kata naki hito wa,
mizukara ie o kobochite
ichi ni idete kore o uru ni,
hitori ga mochiidetaru atai,
nao ichi-nichi ga inochi o sasauru ni dani
oyobazu to zo.

Ayashiki koto wa,
kakaru maki no naka ni, nitsuki,
shirogane kogane no haku nado
tokorodokoro ni tsukite
miyuru ki no ware aimajireri.

The Famine of the Yōwa Era, by Reginald Jackson.

Asking around, I found that people were breaking into old temples and stealing the Buddhas.

They had removed hall fittings and broken them into bits.

I regret being born in such a sinful time,
Witnessing so many dreadful things.

So much heartbreak.

Among loving couples,
The one who loved the deepest was always the first to die.

これを尋ぬればすべき方なきもの、、
古寺に至りて佛をぬすみ、

堂の物の具をやぶりとりて、
わりくだけるなりけり。

濁惡の世にしも生れあひて、
かゝる心うきわざをなむ見侍りし。

又あはれなること侍き。

さりがたき女男など持ちたるものは、
その思ひまさりて、
心ざし深きはかならずさきだちて死しぬ。

Kore o tazunureba subeki katanaki mono no,
koji ni itarite Hotoke o nusumi,

Dō no mono no gu o yaburitorite,
warikudakeru nari keri.

Jokuaku no yo ni shi mo umareaite,
kakaru kokoro ukiwaza o namu mihaberishi.

Mata aware naru koto hebeki.

Sarigataki jodan nado mochitaru mono wa,
sono omoi masarite,
kokorozashi fukaki wa kanarazu sakidachite shishinu.

They sacrificed themselves,
Men and women alike,
Giving what meager food they had to their loved one.

In families, of course,
parents always went first.

I saw babies at the breast,
Unaware that their mothers had perished.

そのゆゑは、我が身をば次になして、
男にもあれ女にもあれ、
いたはしく思ふかたに、
たまたま乞ひ得たる物を、
まづゆづるによりてなり。

されば父子あるものはさだまれる事にて、
親ぞさきだちて死にける。

又母が命つきて臥せるをもしらずして、
いとけなき子の、
その乳房に吸ひつきつつ、
ふせるなどもありけり。

Sono yue wa, wagami o ba tsugi ni nashite,
otoko ni mo are onna ni mo are,
itawashiku omou kata ni,
tamatama koietaru mono o,
mazu yuzuru ni yorite nari.

Sareba fushi aru mono wa sadamareru koto ni te,
oya zo sakidachite shinikeru.

Mata haha ga inochi tsukite fuseru o mo shirazu shite,
itokenaki ko no,
sono chibusa ni suitsukitsutsu,
fuseru nado mo arikeri.

The monk Ryūgyō, who was imperial treasurer
and abbot of the subtemple of Jison'in at Ninnaji,
Felt great pity for the countless dying.

When he noticed a dying person,
He would trace the holy mark upon their forehead,
Binding them to salvation.[11]

During the fourth and fifth months,
He counted forty-two thousand, three hundred dead along
the streets of the capital.
    From Ichijō in the north to Kujō in the south,
    From Kyōgoku in the east to Suzaku in the west.[12]

仁和寺に、慈尊院の大藏卿隆曉法印といふ人、かくしつゝ、數しらず死ぬることをかなしみて、ひじりをあまたかたらひつゝ、その死首の見ゆるごとに、額に阿字を書きて、縁をむすばしむるわざをなむせられける。

その人數を知らむとて、四五兩月がほどかぞへたりければ、京の中、一條より南、九條より北、京極より西、朱雀より東、道のほとりにある頭、すべて四萬二千三百あまりなむありける。

Ninnaji ni,
Jison'in no ōkura kyō Ryūgyō hōin toiu hito,
kakushitsutsu,
kazu shirazu shinuru koto o kanashimite,
hijiri o amata kataraitsutsu,
sono shinikubi no miyuru goto ni,
hitai ni aji o kakite,
en o musubashimuru waza o namuserarekeru.

Sono hitokazu o shiramu to te,
shi-go ryōgetsu ga hodo kazoetarikereba,
miyako no naka, Ichijō yori minami, Kujō yori kita,
Kyōgoku yori nishi, Suzaku yori higashi,
michi no hotori ni aru atama,
subete yon-man ni-sen san-byaku amari namu arikeru.

That total does not include those who perished before or since.

And then there were the countless who died along the riverbed and in the suburbs of Shirakawa and the capital's west.[13]

There were even more along the seven roads leading to the provinces.[14]

I heard there was a similar famine,
In the Chōshō era,*
During the reign of Emperor Sūtoku.[15]

But I know nothing of that age.

All I know is that the more recent famine,
Was the worst I've ever seen before or since.

---

*1132–1135

いはむやその前後に死ぬるもの多く、
河原、白河、にしの京、
もろもろの邊地などをくはへていはゞ
際限もあるべからず。

いかにいはむや、諸國七道をや。

近くは崇徳院の御位のとき、
長承のころかとよ、
かゝるためしはありけると聞けど、
その世のありさまは知らず。

まのあたりいとめづらかに、
かなしかりしことなり。

Iwamuya sono zengo ni shinuru mono ōku,
kawara, Shirakawa, Nishinokyō,
moromoro no henchi nado o kuwaete iwaba
saigen mo arubekarazu.

Ika ni iwamuya, shokoku shichidō o ya.

Chikaku wa Sūtoku'in no mikurai no toki,
Chōshō no koro ka to yo,
kakaru tameshi wa arikeru to kikedo,
sono yo no arisama wa shirazu.

Ma no atari ito mezurakani,
kanashikarishi koto nari.

5
The Earthquake of the Genryaku Era

There was a great earthquake in the second year of the
Genryaku era*.[16]

It was unlike any before.

Mountains crumbled,
Filling rivers with rubble.

The seas heaved,
Engulfing the land.[17]

The ground split open,
And water gushed out.

Boulders cleaved,
Tumbling into valleys below.

Boats along the shore,
Were helpless in the waves.

Horses on the streets,
Stumbled as they walked.

---

*1185

元暦の震災

また元暦二年のころ、
おほなゐふること侍りき。

そのさまよのつねならず。

山くづれて川を埋み、
海かたぶきて陸をひたせり。

土さけて水わきあがり、
いはほわれて谷にまろび入り、
なぎさこぐふねは浪にたゞよひ、
道ゆく駒は足のたちどをまどはせり。

Genryaku no shinsai

Mata Genryaku ni-nen no koro,
ōnai furu koto haberiki.

Sono samayo no tsune narazu.

Yama kuzurete kawa o uzumi,
umi katabukite riku o hitaseri.

Tsuchi sakete mizu wakiagari,
iwa o warete tani ni marobiiri,
nagisa kogu fune wa nami ni tadayoi,
michi yuku koma wa ashi no tachido o madowaseri.

Throughout the capital,
Not a single temple or pagoda remained standing.

Dust and ashes rose up,
Smoke billowed.

The earth roiled,
Houses creaked.

Noise like the sound of thunder.

Those who stayed inside,
They were crushed by their homes.

Those who tried to run,
They were swallowed by the earth.

いはむや都のほとりには、
在々所々堂舎廟塔、
一つとして全からず。

或はくづれ、
或はたふれたぬる間、
塵灰立ちあがりて盛なる煙のごとし。

地のふるひ家のやぶるゝ音、
いかづちにことならず。

家の中に居れば忽にうち
ひしげなむとす。

はしり出づればまた地われさく。

羽なければ空へもあがるべからず。

Iwamuya miyako no hotori ni wa,
zaizai shosho dōsha byōtō,
hitotsu toshite mattakarazu.

Aru wa kuzure,
aru wa taoretanuru aida,
jinkai tachiagarite sakari naru kemuri no gotoshi.

Chi no furui ie no yabururu oto,
ikazuchi ni kotonarazu.

Ie no naka ni ireba niwaka ni uchi
hishigenamu to su.

Hashiriizureba mata chi waresaku.

Hane nakereba sora e mo agarubekarazu.

Having no wings, we can't fly away,
Only a dragon can ride the clouds.

Surely, earthquakes like this are the most terrifying of all
calamities.

An official's child of about six or seven years,
Had built himself a hut at the base of an earthen wall.

He was amusing himself when the wall suddenly collapsed.

Buried under the rubble,
Flat and shapeless, his eyes had popped right out of their
sockets.

龍ならねば雲にのぼらむこと難し。

おそれの中におそるべかりけるは、
たゞ地震なりけるとぞ覺え侍りし。

その中に、あるものゝふのひとり子の、
六つ七つばかりに侍りしが、
ついぢのおほひの下に小家をつくり、
はかなげなるあとなしごとをして
遊び侍りしが、
俄にくづれうめられて、
あとかたなくひらにうちひさがれて、
二つの目など一寸ばかり
うち出されたるを、

Ryū naraneba kumo ni noboramu koto katashi.

Osore no naka ni osorubekarikeru wa,
Tada jishin narikeru to zo oboehaberishi.

Sono naka ni, aru mononofu no hitoriko no,
muttsu nanatsu bakari ni haberishi ga,
tsuiji no ōi no moto ni koya o tsukuri,
hakanagenaru ato nashi goto o shite
asobihaberishi ga,
niwaka ni kuzureumerarete,
atokatanaku hira ni uchihisagarete,
futatsu no me nado issun bakari
uchidasaretaru o,

His parents embraced his lifeless body,
Their unrestrained cries, unbearable.

It was pitiful to see a brave man stricken by grief,
Forgetting his dignity,
Lamenting the loss of his son.

The worst of the shaking didn't go on forever,
But aftershocks continued.

Each of the twenty or thirty aftershocks would have been
frightening enough in normal times.

父母かゝへて、
聲もをしまずかなしみあひて
侍りしこそあはれにかなしく見はべりしか。

子のかなしみにはたけきものも恥を
忘れけりと覺えて、
いとほしくことわりかなとぞ見はべりし。

かくおびたゝしくふることはしばしにて
止みにしかども、
そのなごりしばしば絶えず。

よのつねにおどろくほどの地震、
二三十度ふらぬ日はなし。

fubo kakaete,
koe mo oshimazu kanashimiaite,
haberishi koso aware ni kanashiku mihaberi shika.

Kono kanashimi ni wa takeki mono mo haji o
wasurekeri to oboete,
itooshiku kotowari kana tozo mihaberishi.

Kaku obitatashiku furu koto wa shibashi ni te,
yami ni shikadomo,
sono nagori shibashiba taezu.

Yono tsune ni odoroku hodo no jishin,
ni-san-jū do furanu hi wa nashi.

They only began to abate after ten or twenty days.

Four or five shocks,
Then two or three,
Then only one every few days.

This continued for about three months.

Of the four elements,
Water, fire, and wind cause damage most frequently.

The earth only sometimes brings calamity.

There was a great quake during the Saikō era.*

Among other things, it toppled the head of the Great Buddha at the temple of Tōdaiji.[18]

十日廿日過ぎにしかば、
やうやうまどほになりて、
或は四五度、二三度、
もしは一日まぜ、二三日に一度など、

大かたそのなごり、
三月ばかりや侍りけむ。

四大種の中に、
水火風はつねに害をなせど、
大地に至りては殊なる變をなさず。

むかし齊衡のころかとよ、
おほなゐふりて、
東大寺の佛のみぐし落ちなどして、

Tōka hatsuka sugi ni shikaba,
yōyō madō ni narite,
aru wa shi- go-do, ni- san-do,
moshi wa ichinichi maze, ni- san-nichi ni ichido nado,

ōkata sono nagori,
mitsuki bakari ya haberikemu.

Shidaishu no naka ni,
mizu hi kaze wa tsune ni gai o nasedo,
daichi ni itarite wa koto naru hen o nasazu.

Mukashi Saikō no koro ka to yo,
ōnai furite,
Tōdaiji no Hotoke no migushi ochi nado shite,

And yet, that disaster was still not as terrible as the earth-quake of Genryaku.

Everyone expressed pathetic thoughts,
As the quake made them examine their hearts,
And reflect on the vanities of this world.

But in the end, as days, months, and years passed,
Not one person remained mindful.

いみじきことゞも侍りけれど、
猶このたびにはしかずとぞ。

すなはち人皆あぢきなきことを述べて、
いさゝか心のにごりもうすらぐと見えしほどに、
月日かさなり年越えしかば、
後は言の葉にかけて、
いひ出づる人だになし。

imijiki koto domo haberikeredo,
nao kono tabi ni wa shikazu to zo.

Sunawachi hito mina ajikinaki koto o nobete,
isasaka kokoro no nigori mo usuragu to mieshi hodo ni,
tsukihi kasanari toshikoe shikaba,
ato wa kotonoha ni kakete,
iiizuru hito dani nashi.

Detachment

6

Where to Find Peace

Life in this world is hard.

As I've been saying,
People and their houses,
Are empty and impermanent.

The demands of status and rank,
They bring countless worries.

The lowly man who lives in the shadow of the powerful:
  He cannot rejoice when glad,

住みにくき世

すべて世のありにくきこと、
わが身とすみかとの、
はかなくあだなるさまかくのごとし。

いはむや所により、
身のほどにしたがひて、
心をなやますこと、
あげてかぞふべからず。

もしおのづから身かずならずして、
權門のかたはらに居るものは深く
悦ぶことあれども、
大にたのしぶにあたはず。

Suminikuki yo

Subete yo no arinikuki koto,
waga mi to sumika to no,
hakanaku adanaru sama kaku no gotoshi.

Iwamuya tokoro ni yori,
mi no hodo ni shitagaite,
kokoro o nayamasu koto,
agete kazoubekarazu.

Moshi onozukara mikazu narazu shite,
kenmon no katawara ni iru mono wa fukaku
yorokobu koto aredomo,
ōi ni tanoshibu ni atawazu.

Or cry out when overcome by sorrow.

It's not easy for him to act freely.

He's like a sparrow near the nest of a hawk:
    Always anxious,
    Always trembling.

The poor man who lives in the shadow of the rich:
    His poverty brings him shame.

Morning or night,
When coming or going,
He must always be obsequious.

なげきある時も、
聲をあげて泣くことなし。

進退やすからず、
たちゐにつけて恐れをの、くさま、
たとへば、
雀の鷹の巣に近づけるがごとし。

もし貧しくして富める家の
隣にをるものは、
朝夕すぼき姿を
恥ぢてへつらひつ、出で入る。

Nageki aru toki mo,
koe o agete naku koto nashi.

Shindai yasukarazu,
tachii ni tsukete osore ononokusama,
tatoeba,
suzume no taka no su ni chikazukeru ga gotoshi.

Moshi mazushiku shite tomeru ie no
tonari ni oru mono wa,
asayū suboki sugata o
hajite hetsuraitsutsu ideiru.

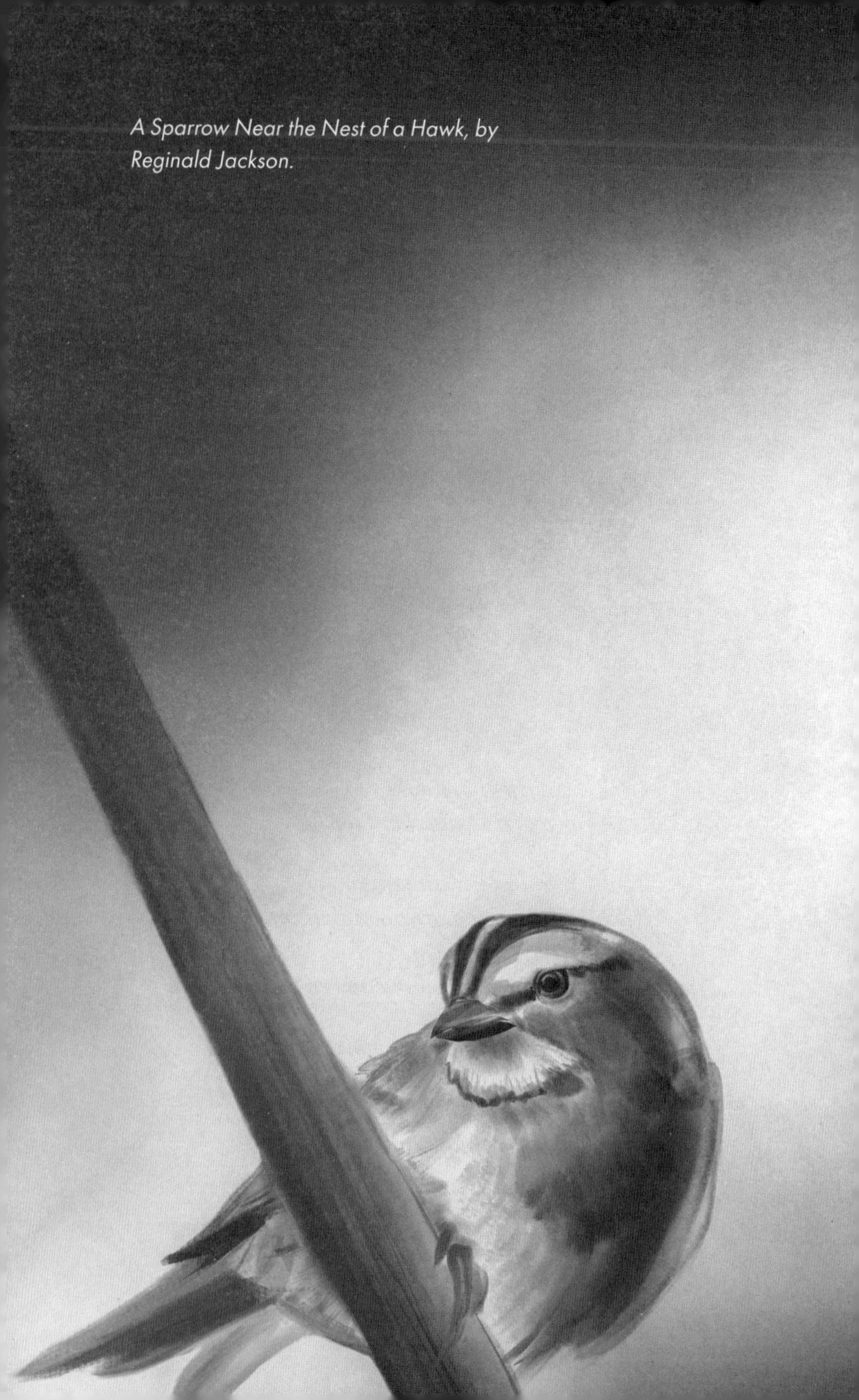

A Sparrow Near the Nest of a Hawk, by Reginald Jackson.

When he notices his wife, children, and pages envying
their rich neighbor,
Or when he hears of that rich neighbor treating them with
contempt,

He can never find peace.

If one lives in a crowded place,
It's impossible to flee when there's a fire.

If one lives on the margins,
Travel is difficult,
And then there's the danger of thieves.

The powerful are greedy!
Those who live apart are mocked.

妻子、僮僕のうらやめるさまを見るにも、
富める家のひとのないがしろなる
けしきを聞くにも、
心念々にうごきて時としてやすからず。

もしせばき地に居れば、
近く炎上する時、
その害をのがる、ことなし。

もし邊地にあれば、
往反わづらひ多く、
盗賊の難はなれがたし。

いきほひあるものは貪欲ふかく、
ひとり身なるものは人にかろしめらる。

Saishi, dōboku no ura yameru sama o miru ni mo,
tomeru ie no hito no naigashiro naru
keshiki o kiku ni mo,
kokoro nennen ni ugokite toki to shite yasukarazu.

Moshi sebakichi ni ireba,
chikaku enjō suru toki,
sono gai o nogaruru koto nashi.

Moshi henchi ni areba,
ōhan wazurai ōku,
tōzoku no nan wa naregatashi.

Ikioi aru mono wa don'yoku fukaku,
hitori mi naru mono wa hito ni karoshimeraru.

Those with wealth have much to fear,
The poor have only bitterness.

If one relies on another,
He becomes dependent.

If he nurtures another,
He becomes attached.

If one conforms to the world,
He's bound to suffer.

If he doesn't,
He's considered mad.

So I ask myself:
    Where in this world should one live and how?
    Where can one find rest,
    And peace in their heart?

寶あればおそれ多く、
貧しければなげき切なり。

人を頼めば身他のやつことなり、
人をはぐくめば心恩愛につかはる。

世にしたがへば身くるし。

またしたがはねば狂へるに似たり。

いづれの所をしめ、
いかなるわざをしてか、
しばしもこの身をやどし玉ゆらも
心をなぐさむべき。

Takara areba osore ōku,
mazushikereba nageki setsunari.

Hito o tanomeba mi hokano yatsuko to nari,
hito o hagukumeba kokoro on'ai ni tsukawaru.

Yo ni shitagaeba mi kurushi.

Mata shitagawaneba kurueru ni nitari.

Izure no tokoro o shime,
ikanaru waza o shite ka,
shibashi mo kono mi o yadoshi tamayura mo
kokoro o nagusamubeki.

7
Leaving the World

I lived and worked for a long time in the household of my
paternal grandmother.

When she died, familial ties were sundered,
And I began to decline.

Although it was a place with many memories,
I could remain there no longer.

At about thirty, I decided to bind my destiny to a her-
mitage.

Although it was one-tenth the size of my birth home,
It was enough for me.

あられぬ世

我が身、父の方の祖母の家をつたへて、久しく彼所に住む。

そののち縁かけ、身おとろへて、しのぶかたがたしげかりしかば、つひにあととむることを得ずして、三十餘にして、更に我が心と一つの庵をむすぶ。

これをありしすまひになずらふるに、十分が一なり。

Ararenu yo

*Waga mi, chichi no kata no sobo no ie o tsutaete,
hisashiku asoko ni sumu.*

*Sono nochi en kake,
mi otoroete,
shinobu katagata shigekarishi kaba,
tsuini ato tomuru koto o ezu shite,
sanjū amari ni shite, sarani waga kokoro to hitotsu no
iori o musubu.*

*Kore o arishisumai ni nazurauru ni,
jūbun ga ich inari.*

It was little more than a shack,
Not a proper house at all.

It had mud walls, but no gate.

I used bamboo pillars to erect a roof over my cart.

When the wind blew or snow fell,
The whole thing felt so precarious.

Being near the riverbank,
Flooding was a constant threat.

Thieves weren't uncommon either.

たゞ居屋ばかりをかまへて、
はかばかしくは屋を造るにおよばず。

わづかについひぢをつけりといへども、
門たつるたづきなし。

竹を柱として車やどりとせり。

雪ふり風吹くごとに、
危ふからずしもあらず。

所は河原近ければ、水の難も深く、
白波のおそれもさわがし。

Tada kyooku bakari o kamaete,
hakabakashiku wa oku o tsukuru ni oyobazu.

Wazuka ni tsuiiji o tsukeri to iedomo,
mon tatsuru tazuki nashi.

Take o hashira to shite kuruma yadori to seri.

Yuki furi kaze fuku goto ni,
ayaukarazu shimoarazu.

Tokoro wa kawara chikakereba, mizu no nan mo fukaku,
shiranami no osore mo sawagashi.

I had lived for over thirty years,
With a heart troubled by this unkind world.

I was nevertheless aware of my good fortune throughout,
Fleeting though it was.

Then, in my fiftieth spring,
I left the bosom of my family,
Turning my back on the world.

After all, I had no wife, no child,
Nothing to ground me.

すべてあらぬ世を念じ過ぐしつゝ、
心をなやませることは、
三十餘年なり。

その間をりをりのたがひめに、
おのづから短き運をさとりぬ。

すなはち五十の春をむかへて、
家を出で世をそむけり。

もとより妻子なければ、
捨てがたきよすがもなし。

Subete aranu yo o nenji sugu shitsutsu,
kokoro o nayamaseru koto wa,
sanjū yo-nen nari.

Sono aida oriori no tagaime ni,
onozukara mijikaki un o satorinu.

Sunawachi gojū no haru o mukaete,
ie o ide yo o somukeri.

Motoyori saishi nakereba,
sutegataki yosuga mo nashi.

I had no rank or income,
No worldly ties to bind me.

For the next five springs and autumns,
I took refuge amidst the clouds of Mt. Ōhara.[19]

身に官禄あらず、
何につけてか執をとゞめむ。
むなしく大原山の雲にふして、
いくそばくの春秋をかへぬる。

Mi ni kanroku arazu,
nani ni tsukete ka shissu o todomemu.

Munashiku Ōhara-yama no kumo ni fushite,
ikusobaku no shunjū o kaenuru.

The Mountains of Ōhara, by Reginald Jackson.

8
My Little Hut

When I had reached the age of sixty,
    —and the dew of life had disappeared—
I built a hut to be my final refuge.

Like a woodsman building a boorish shelter,
Or an old silkworm spinning his last cocoon.

My new hut is not even a hundredth the size of my last.

As I get older,
My abode gets smaller.

仮の庵のありよう

こゝに六十の露消えがたに及びて、
さらに末葉のやどりを結べることあり。

いはゞ狩人のひとよの宿をつくり、
老いたるかひこのまゆをいとなむがごとし。

これを中ごろのすみかになずらふれば、
また百分が一にだもおよばず。

とかくいふ程に、
よはひは年々にかたぶき、
すみかはをりをりにせばし。

Kari no io no ariyō

Koko ni rokujū no tsuyu kiegata ni oyobite,
sarani uraba no yadori o musuberu koto ari.

Iwaba kariudo no hitoyo no yado o tsukuri,
oitaru kaiko no mayu o itonamu ga gotoshi.

Kore o nakagoro no sumika ni nazuraureba,
mata hyakubun ga ichi ni da mo oyobazu.

Tokaku iu hodo ni,
yowai wa nennen ni katabuki,
sumika wa oriori ni sebashi.

This one's unique:
    It's a *hōjō*, a hut measuring just three meters to a side,
    No more than two meters tall.[20]

I built it on a random plot,
Staking no claim to the land.

I thatched it simply,
Clamping the joints together with metal hasps.

Building in this way makes transport easy,
Should I ever wish to move.

その家のありさまよのつねにも似ず。

廣さはわづかに方丈、
高さは七尺が内なり。

所をおもひ定めざるがゆゑに、
地をしめて造らず。

土居をくみ、うちおほひをふきて、
つぎめごとにかけがねをかけたり。

もし心にかなはぬことあらば、
やすく外へうつさむがためなり。

Sono ie no arisama yo no tsune ni mo nizu.

*Hirosa wa wazuka ni hōjō,
takasa wa nanashaku ga uchi nari.*

*Tokoro o omoisadamezaru ga yue ni,
chi o shimete tsukurazu.*

*Doi o kumi, uchiōi o fukite,
tsugimegotoni kakegane o kaketari.*

*Moshi kokoro ni kanawanu koto araba,
yasuku hoka e utsusamu ga tame nari.*

Rebuilding won't be difficult either:
    The whole thing can fit into two carts,
    And the only cost will be the carter's fee.

I hide myself away,
Deep in the hills of Hino.[21]

Along the south wall of my hut,
I erected a temporary awning,
And laid out a bamboo duckboard.

To the west, I built a ritual cabinet.

Along the western wall,
I've enshrined an image of Amida.

When bathed in evening light,
A warm glow emanates from Amida's forehead.[22]

そのあらため造るとき、
いくばくのわづらひかある。

積むところわづかに二輌なり。

車の力をむくゆるほかは、
更に他の用途いらず。

いま日野山の奥にあとをかくして後、
南にかりの日がくしをさし出して、
竹のすのこを敷き、
その西に閼伽棚を作り、
うちには西の垣に添へて、

阿彌陀の畫像を安置したてまつりて、
落日をうけて、眉間のひかりとす。

Sono aratame tsukuru toki,
ikubaku no wazurai ka aru.

Tsumu tokoro wazuka ni niryō nari.

Kuruma no chikara o mukuyuru hoka wa,
sara ni hoka no yōto irazu.

Ima Hinoyama no oku ni ato o kakushite nochi,
minami ni kari no higakushi o sashidashite,
take no sunoko o shiki,
sono nishi ni akadana o tsukuri,
uchi ni wa nishi no kaki ni soete,

Amida no gazō o anchi shitatematsurite,
rakujitsu o ukete, miken no hikari to su.

On the doors of his tabernacle,
There are images of the bodhisattvas Fugen and Fudō.[23]

On the north side of my hut,
Upon a shelf above the sliding doors,
I've placed three or four black, leather-lined baskets.

Inside, I keep my poetry and music,
Along with various writings,
Like Genshin's *Essentials of Rebirth in the Pure Land*.[24]

Next to that is a lute and a Japanese zither,
They're known as the "jointed lute" and "folding zither."

かの帳のとびらに、
普賢ならびに不動の像をかけたり。

北の障子の上に、
ちひさき棚をかまへて、
黒き皮篭三四合を置く。

すなはち和歌、管絃、
往生要集ごときの抄物を入れたり。

傍にこと、琵琶、おのおの一張をたつ。

いはゆるをりごと、つき琵琶これなり。

Kano tobari no tobira ni,
Fugen narabi ni Fudō no zō o kaketari.

Kitano shoji no ue ni,
chiisaki tana o kamaete,
kuroki kawago san-shi gō o oku.

Sunawachi waka, kangen,
Ōjōyōshū gotoki no shōmono o iretari.

Katawara ni koto, biwa, onoono icchō o tatsu.

Iwayuru ori-goto, tsuki-biwa kore nari.

In the east,
I've laid out some dried bracken for a bed.

Along that wall opens a window,
Where I've placed an attached writing desk.

Near my pillow is a brazier,
Where I burn brushwood.

North of the hut is a little plot surrounded by a low hedge:
  That's where I grow medicinal herbs.

東にそへて、わらびのほどろを敷き、つかなみを敷きて夜の床とす。

東の垣に窓をあけて、こゝにふづくゑを出せり。

枕の方にすびつあり。

これを柴折りくぶるよすがとす。

庵の北に少地をしめ、あばらなるひめ垣をかこひて園とす。

すなはちもろもろの薬草をうゑたり。

Higashi ni soete, warabi no hodoro o shiki,
tsukanami o shikite yoru no toko to su.

Higashi no kaki ni mado o akete,
koko ni fuzukue o daseri.

Makura no kata ni subitsu ari.

Kore o shibaori kuburu yosu ga to su.

Iori no kita ni shōchi o shime,
abara naru himegaki o kakoite en to su.

Sunawachi moromoro no yakusō o uetari.

Kamo no Chōmei's Mountain Home (his *hōjō*) in the hills of Toyama, by Reginald Jackson.

Such is my temporary abode in this world.

Outside to the south,
A pipe draws water into a basin made of stones.

The woods nearby provide firewood in abundance.

The hills are called Toyama.

Thick jasmine conceals my every trace.

The valley below is overgrown,
But I have a clear view to the west,
The direction I face when praying.

かりの庵のありさまかくのごとし。

その所のさまをいはゞ、
南にかけひあり、
岩をたゝみて水をためたり。

林軒近ければ、
つま木を拾ふにともしからず。

名を外山といふ。

まさきのかづらあとをうづめり。

谷しげゝれど、
にしは晴れたり。

観念のたよりなきにしもあらず。

Kari no io no arisama kaku no gotoshi.

Sono tokoro no sama o iwaba,
minami ni kakei ari,
iwa o tatamite mizu o tametari.

Rinken chikakereba,
tsumaki o hirou ni to mo shikarazu.

Na o Toyama to iu.

Masaki no kazura ato o uzumeri.

Tani shigekeredo,
nishi wa haretari.

Kannen no tayori naki ni shimo arazu.

In the spring, I see wisteria flowers,
Bloom like purple clouds in the west.[25]

In summer,
The chattering cuckoos guide me,
Toward the mountain pass of death.

In the autumn,
The cries of cicadas at dusk fill my ears,
Lamenting this empty husk of a world.

In winter,
Snow covers the earth.

It accumulates then melts away,
Like sin and its redemption.

春は藤なみを見る、
紫雲のごとくして西のかたに匂ふ。

夏は郭公をきく、かたらふごとに
死出の山路をちぎる。

秋は日ぐらしの聲耳に充てり。

うつせみの世をかなしむかと聞ゆ。

冬は雪をあはれむ。

つもりきゆるさま、
罪障にたとへつべし。

Haru wa fuji nami o miru,
shiun no gotoku shite nishi no kata ni niou.

Natsu wa kakkō o kiku, katarau goto ni
shide no yamaji o chigiru.

Aki wa higurashi no koe mimi ni ateri.

Utsusemi no yo o kanashimu ka to kikoyu.

Fuyu wa yuki o awaremu.

Tsumorikiyuru sama,
zaishō ni tatoetsubeshi.

When I'm in no mood for reciting or reading sutras,
I rest.

I can be lazy if I want:
    There's no one here to stop me,
    No friends to pass judgement.

Although I took no vow of silence,
Being alone means there's nothing to say.

It's not hard to keep the holy precepts,
There's little chance of breaking them.

In the mornings when my heart is full of that feeling,
Like the "white-crested wake that rises astern,"
I gaze out upon the boats that ply the river near Okanoya,
And write in the manner of Manshami.[26]

もしねんぶつものうく、
どきやうまめならざる時は、
みづから休み、
みづからをこたるにさまたぐる
人もなく、また恥づべき友もなし。

殊更に無言をせざれども、
ひとり居ればくごふををさめつべし。

必ず禁戒をまもるともしもなけれども、
境界なければ何につけてか破らむ。

もしあとの白波に身をよする
あしたには、
岡のやに行きかふ船をながめて、
滿沙彌が風情をぬすみ、

Moshi nenbutsu mono uku,
dokyō mamenarazaru toki wa,
mizukara yasumi,
mizukara okotaru ni samataguru
hito mo naku, mata hazubeki tomo mo nashi.

Kotosara ni mugon o sezaredomo,
hitori ireba kugou o osametsubeshi.

Kanarazu kinkai o mamoru to shi mo nakeredomo,
kyōkai nakereba nani ni tsukete ka yaburamu.

Moshi ato no shiranami ni mi o yosuru
ashita ni wa,
Okanoya ni ikikau fune o nagamete,
Manshami ga fuzei o nusumi,

121

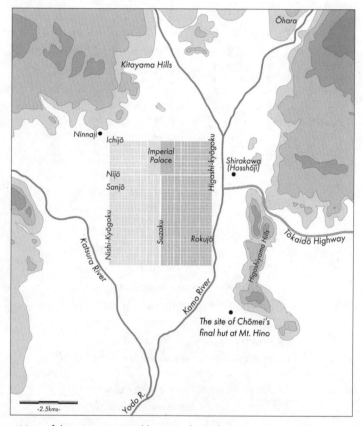

Map of the greater capital basin in the 13th century, showing key sites mentioned in *Hōjōki*, including Ōhara, Hino, Shirakawa, the Yodo River, and the temple of Ninnaji. The temple of Ishiyama-dera is to the south-east of the map area.

In the evening when the wind blows hard,
Making the leaves of the judas trees dance,
I think of the Xunyang River,
And pretend that I'm Minamoto no Tsunenobu.[27]

When I'm in the mood,
I play the "Song of Autumn Breezes,"
To the wind in the pines,
Or "Flowing Water" to the babble of the stream.[28]

Although I'm not skilled,
I play not to please the ears of another.

I play and sing on my own,
To give sustenance to my heart alone.

もし桂の風、葉をならすゆふべには、
潯陽の江をおもひやりて、
源都督（經信）のながれをならふ。

もしあまりの興あれば、
しばしば松のひゞきに秋風の樂をたぐへ、
水の音に流泉の曲をあやつる。

藝はこれつたなけれども、
人の耳を悦ばしめむとにもあらず。

ひとりしらべ、ひとり詠じて、
みづから心を養ふばかりなり。

moshi katsura no kaze, ha o narasu yūbe ni wa,
Jin'yō no e o omoiyarite,
Gen Totoku (Tsunenobu) no nagare o narau.

Moshi amari no kyō areba,
shibashiba matsu no hibiki ni Akikaze no gaku wo tague,
mizu no oto ni Ryūsen no kyoku o ayatsuru.

Gei wa kore tsutanakeredomo,
hito no mimi o yorokobashimemu to ni mo arazu.

Hitori shirabe, hitori eijite,
mizukara kokoro wo yashinau bakari nari.

9
Finding Contentment

There's another timber hut at the base of the mountain:
   It's home to the woodsman.

His son visits me sometimes.

When all is still,
We go for walks.

He's sixteen and I, sixty.

Despite the age gap,
We derive much joy from each other's company.

草庵の生活

また麓に一つの柴の庵あり。

すなはちこの山もりが居る所なり。

かしこに小童あり。

時々來りてあひとぶらふ。

もしつれづれなる時は、
これを友としてあそびありく。

かれは十六歳、われは六十、
その齢ことの外なれど、
心を慰むることはこれおなじ。

Sōan no seikatsu

Mata fumoto ni hitotsu no shiba no iori ari.

Sunawachi kono yamamori ga iru tokoro nari.

Kashiko ni kowarawa ari.

Tokidoki kitarite aitoburau.

Moshi tsurezure naru toki wa,
kore o tomo to shite asobiariku.

Kare wa jūroku-sai, ware wa rokujū,
sono yowai koto no hoka naredo,
kokoro o nagusamuru koto wa kore onaji.

We pull up pampas grass,
And pick mayflowers.

Pile up yam buds,
And break off water dropwort.

Or we head to the paddy reservoirs below,
Gathering fallen rice stalks,
Weaving them into different shapes.

When the weather is fine,
We clamber to the top of the hill,
To gaze at the sky above my former home.

We can see Mt. Kohata,
The villages of Fushimi, Toba, and Hatsukashi.[29]

Nothing can dint our pleasure,
Because a place of beauty has no owner.

あるはつばなをぬき、
いはなしをとりり。

またぬかごをもり、
芹をつむ。

或はすそわの田井に至りて、
おちほを拾ひてほぐみをつくる。

もし日うらゝかなれば、
嶺によぢのぼりて、
はるかにふるさとの空を望み、
木幡山、伏見の里、鳥羽、
羽束師を見る。

勝地はぬしなければ、
心を慰むるにさはりなし。

Aru wa tsubana o nuki,
iwanashi o toriri.

Mata nukago o mori,
seri o tsumu.

Aru wa susowa no tai ni itarite,
ochiho o hiroite hogumi o tsukuru.

Moshi hi urarakanareba,
mine ni yojinoborite,
haruka ni furusato no sora o nozomi,
Kohatayama, Fushiminosato, Toba,
Hatsukashi o miru.

Shōchi wa nushi nakereba,
kokoro o nagusamuru ni sawari nashi.

When we have the energy,
And feel like venturing further afield,
We hike eastward through the hills, past Sumiyama,
Kasatori, and Ishima,
Offering prayers at the temple of Ishiyama-dera.[30]

Or we cross the fields of Awazu,
To visit the former home of the venerable Semimaru.

Sometimes we cross the Tanakami River,
Paying our respects at the grave of Sarumaro.

On our way home, and depending on the season,
We might view cherry blossoms or autumn leaves.

We pluck bracken or gather nuts,
Either to offer to the Buddha or to keep for ourselves.

あゆみわづらひなく、
志遠くいたる時は、
これより峯つゞき炭山を越え、
笠取を過ぎて、石間にまうで、
或は石山ををがむ。

もしは、粟津の原を分けて、
蝉丸翁が迹をとぶらひ、
田上川をわたりて、
猿丸大夫が墓をたづぬ。

歸るさには、をりにつけつゝ櫻をかり、
紅葉をもとめ、わらびを折り、
木の實を拾ひて、
かつは佛に奉りかつは家づとにす。

Ayumi wazurainaku,
kokorozashi tōku itaru toki wa,
kore yori mine tsuzuki Sumiyama o koe,
Kasatori wo sugite, Ishima ni mōde,
aru wa Ishiyama o ogamu.

Moshi wa, Awazu no hara o wakete,
Semimaru okina ga ato o toburai,
Tanakamigawa o watarite,
Sarumaro daifu ga haka o tazunu.

Kaeru sa ni wa, ori ni tsuketsutsu sakura o kari,
momiji o motome, warabi o ori,
ki no mi o hiroite,
katsu wa Hotoke tatematsuri katsu wa iezuto ni su.

When the night is quiet,
I think of the departed,
Wetting my sleeves to a chorus of chattering monkeys.

Fireflies in the bushes,
Resemble fishermen's braziers off the island of
Makinoshima.[31]

The rain at daybreak,
Feels like a storm pelting the leaves.

The throaty warbles of copper pheasants,
Remind me of the voices of my mother and father.

When mountain deer approach me without fear,
I realize just how far removed from the world I've become.

もし夜しづかなれば、
窓の月に故人を忍び、
猿の聲に袖をうるほす。

くさむらの螢は、
遠く眞木の島の篝火にまがひ、
曉の雨は、
おのづから木の葉吹くあらしに似たり。

山鳥のほろほろと鳴くを聞きても、
父か母かとうたがひ、
みねのかせきの近くなれたるにつけても、
世にとほざかる程を知る。

Moshi yoru shizuka nareba,
mado no tsuki ni kojin o shinobi,
saru no koe ni sode o uruosu.

Kusamura no hotaru wa,
tōku Makinoshima no kagaribi ni magai,
akatsuki no ame wa,
onozukara konoha fuku arashi ni nitari.

Yamadori no horohoro to naku o kikite mo,
chichi ka haha ka to utagai,
mine no kaseki no chikaku naretaru ni tsukete mo,
yo ni tōzakaru hodo o shiru.

The embers I poke in the fire,
Like friends, they signal the dawn of my twilight years.

Although the mountains can be forbidding,
I enjoy the hooting of owls.

Each season is enchanting in its own way.

A more perceptive, deeper man than I,
Would surely discover even more beauty.

When I first came to the mountains,
I did not plan to stay long.

And yet here I am,
Five years later.

或は埋火をかきおこして、
老の寝覺の友とす。

おそろしき山ならねど、
ふくろふの聲をあはれむにつけても、
山中の景氣、
折につけてつくることなし。

いはむや深く思ひ、
深く知れらむ人のためには、
これにしもかぎるべからず。

大かた此所に住みそめしは、
あからさまとおもひしかど、
今までに五とせを經たり。

Aru wa uzumibi o kakiokoshite,
oi no nezame no tomo to su.

Osoroshiki yama naranedo,
fukurō no koe o awaremu ni tsukete mo,
sanchū no keiki,
ori ni tsukete tsukuru koto nashi.

Iwamuya fukaku omoi,
fukaku shireramu hito no tame ni wa,
kore ni shi mo kagirubekarazu.

Ōkata koko ni sumisomeshi wa,
akarasama to omoishikado,
ima made ni go to se o hetari.

This aging, temporary shelter,
Has become my home.

Rotting leaves on the eves,
Blanketed in moss.

I sometimes receive word from the capital:
    While I've been here in the hills,
    Many ranking lords have died.

The departed of more humble status,
They're too numerous to count.

Just how many houses have been lost to the constant fires?

假の庵もやゝふる屋となりて、
軒にはくちばふかく、
土居に苔むせり。

おのづから事とのたよりに都を聞けば、
この山にこもり居て後、
やごとなき人の、
かくれ給へるもあまた聞ゆ。

ましてその数ならぬたぐひ、
つくしてこれを知るべからず。

たびたびの炎上にほろびたる家、
またいくそばくぞ。

Kari no io mo yaya furuya to narite,
noki ni wa kuchiba fukaku,
doi ni koke museri.

Onozukara koto to no tayori ni miyako o kikeba,
kono yama ni komoriite nochi,
yagotonaki hito no,
kakuretamaeru mo amata kikoyu.

Mashite sono kazu naranu tagui,
tsukushite kore o shirubekarazu.

Tabitabi no enjō ni horobitaru ie,
mata ikusobaku zo.

Nothing happens here,
In my temporary hut.

Small as it is,
There's room enough to sleep at night and to sit by day:
    More than enough for one man.

The hermit crab likes a tiny shell,
Because it knows itself so well.

The osprey lives on the rocky coast,
Because it fears the world of man.

たゞかりの庵のみ、
のどけくしておそれなし。

ほどせばしといへども、
夜臥す床あり、
ひる居る座あり。

一身をやどすに不足なし。

がうなはちひさき貝をこのむ、
これよく身をしるによりて
なり。

みさごは荒磯に居る、
則ち人をおそるゝが故
なり。

Tada kari no io nomi,
nodokeku shite osore nashi.

Hodosebashi to iedomo,
yoru fusu toko ari,
hiru iru za ari.

Isshin o yadosu ni fusoku nashi.

Gōna wa chiisaki kai o konomu,
kore yoku mi o shiru ni yorite nari.

Misago wa araiso ni iru,
sunawachi hito o osoruru ga yue nari.

So it is with me:
    I know myself,
    And I know the world.

I wish for nothing,
And seek not to conform.

Quietude is all I desire:
    To be free from worry is happiness enough.

People in this world don't build houses to meet their needs.

They build them to keep wives, children, and retinues.

Some build to impress their friends and acquaintances,
To provide lodging to a lord or teacher.

Some, of course, are simply housing their treasures:
    Oxen and horses.

我またかくのごとし。

身を知り世を知れらば、
願はずまじらはず、
たゞしづかなるをのぞみとし、
うれへなきをたのしみとす。

すべて世の人の、
すみかを作るならひ、
かならずしも身のためにはせず。

或は妻子眷屬のために作り、
或は親昵朋友のために作る。

或は主君、師匠、および財寶、
馬牛のためにさへこれをつくる。

Ware mata kaku no gotoshi.

Mi o shiri yo o shireraba,
negawazu majirawazu,
tada shizuka naru o nozomi to shi,
uree naki o tanoshimi to su.

Subete yo no hito no,
sumika o tsukuru narai,
kanarazushimo mi no tame ni wa sezu.

Aru ha saishi kenzoku no tame ni tsukuri,
aru wa shinjitsu hōyū no tame ni tsukuru.

Aru wa shukun, shishō, oyobi zaihō,
uma ushi no tame ni sae kore o tsukuru.

I built for myself alone.

You may wonder why.

The world today has its ways,
And I have mine.

I have no companion nor servant.

Even if I built a bigger house,
Who would I welcome?
With whom would I share it?

我今、身のためにむすべり。

人のために作らず。

ゆゑいかんとなれば、今の世のならひ、
この身のありさま、ともなふべき人もなく、
たのむべきやつこもなし。

たとひ廣く作れりとも、
誰をかやどし、
誰をかすゑん。

Ware ima, mi no tame ni musuberi.

Hito no tame ni tsukurazu.

Yue ikan to nareba, ima no yo no narai,
kono mi no arisama, tomonaubeki hito mo naku,
tanomubeki yatsuko mo nashi.

Tatoi hiroku tsukureri to mo,
dare o ka yadoshi,
dare o ka suen.

10
Self-Reliance

In their friends,
People like to find affluence and a ready smile.

Compassion and honesty,
Not so much.

So why not make friends with music and nature instead:
    The moon; the flowers?

Servants are preoccupied with rewards and punishments,
Venerating generous favors the most.

自力更生

それ人の友たるものは富めるをたふとみ、
ねんごろなるを先とす。

かならずしも、
情あると、
すぐなるとをば愛せず。

たゞ絲竹花月を友とせむにはしかじ。

人のやつこたるものは
賞罰のはなはだしきを顧み、
恩の厚きを重くす。

Jiriki kōsei

Sore hito no tomo taru mono wa tomeru o tōtomi,
nengoro naru o saki to su.

Kanarazushimo,
nasake aru to,
sugunaru to o ba ai sezu.

Tada shichiku kuwagetsu o tomo to semu ni wa shikaji.

Hito no yatsuko taru mono wa
shōbatsu no hanahadashiki o kaerimi,
on no atsuki o omokusu.

145

Although I'm mindful of the particles
that make up my being,
I seek not easy idleness.[32]

If something needs doing,
Why not be your own servant?

True, it requires effort,
But it's better than being obliged to another.

When you need to go somewhere, walk.

更にはごくみあはれぶといへども、
やすく閑なるをばねがはず、
たゞ我が身を奴婢とするにはしかず。

もしなすべきことあれば、
すなはちおのづから身をつかふ。

たゆからずしもあらねど、
人をしたがへ、
人をかへりみるよりはやすし。

もしありくべきことあれば、
みづから歩む。

Sarani wa gokumi awarebu to iedomo,
yasuku hima naru o ba negawazu,
tada waga mi o doi to suru ni wa shikazu.

Moshi nasubeki koto areba,
sunawachi onozukara mi o tsukau.

Tayukarazu shi mo aranedo,
hito o shitagae,
hito o kaerimiru yori wa yasushi.

Moshi arikubeki koto areba,
mizukara ayumu.

Sure, even that can be hard,
But it's not as hard as always having to worry about horse
and saddle, ox and cart.

This one body has a dual purpose:
   My hands do my work,
   My legs get me around.

I know my own limits.

I'll rest when it pleases me,
And work again when I wish.

くるしといへども、
馬鞍牛車と心をなやますにはしかず。

今ひと身をわかちて。

二つの用をなす。

手のやつこ、
足ののり物、
よくわが心にかなへり。

心また身のくるしみを知れゝば、
くるしむ時はやすめつ、
まめなる時はつかふ。

Kurushi to iedomo,
uma kura ushi kuruma to kokoro o nayamasu ni wa shikazu.

Ima hitomi o wakachite.

Futatsu no yō o nasu.

Te no yatsuko,
ashi no norimono,
yoku waga kokoro ni kanaeri.

Kokoro mata mi no kurushimi o shirereba,
kurushimu toki wa yasumetsu,
mame naru toki wa tsukau.

I exert myself,
But never to excess.

So even when fatigued,
I'm not distressed.

Always walking,
Always working,
I foster a robust spirit.

Why rest when I don't need to?

It's a sin to cause others to suffer or worry.

Isn't it better to expend one's energy in other ways?

つかふとても、
たびたび過さず。

ものうしとても心をうごかすことなし。

いかにいはむや、
常にありき、
常に働くは、
これ養生なるべし。

なんぞいたづらにやすみ居らむ。

人を苦しめ、
人を悩ますはまた罪業なり。

いかゞ他の力をかるべき。

Tsukau to te mo,
tabitabi sugosazu.

Mono ushi to te mo kokoro o ugokasu koto nashi.

Ikani iwamuya,
tsune ni ariki,
tsune ni hataraku wa,
kore yōjō naru beshi.

Nanzo itazura ni yasumi iramu.

Hito o kurushime,
hito o nayamasu wa mata zaigō nari.

Ikaga hoka no chikara o karubeki.

11
Simplicity

The same principle of self-sufficiency applies to food and clothing.

I make do with what I can source myself:
    My clothes are woven wisteria,
    My bedding, made from hemp.

Tender shoots from the fields and berries from the hills:
    They're all I need for sustenance.

Because I don't mingle with others,
My appearance doesn't matter.

The simpler my food,
The sweeter it tastes.

足るを知る

衣食のたぐひまたおなじ。

藤のころも、
麻のふすま、
得るに隨ひてはだへをかくし。

野邊のつばな、
嶺の木の實、
わづかに命をつぐばかりなり。

人にまじらはざれば、
姿を恥づる悔もなし。

かてともしければおろそか
なれども、なほ味をあまくす。

Taru o shiru

Ishoku no tagui mata onaji.

Fuji no koromo,
asa no fusuma,
eru ni shitagaite hadae o kakushi.

Nobe no tsubana,
mine no ki no mi,
wazuka ni inochi o tsugu bakari nari.

Hito ni majirawazareba,
sugata o hazuru kai mo nashi.

Kate tomoshikereba orosoka
naredomo, nao aji o amakusu.

What I'm saying doesn't apply to all the merry rich.

I'm merely comparing my current and former lives.

To leave this world and reject the cares of the flesh,
Is to live without bitterness or fear.

I commend my life to the Will of Heaven,
Without regret or bitterness.

I think of my body like a floating cloud,
Never trusting nor despising it.

すべてかやうのこと、
樂しく富める人に對していふにはあらず。

たゞわが身一つにとりて、
昔と今とをたくらぶるばかりなり。

大かた世をのがれ、
身を捨てしより、
うらみもなくおそれもなし。

命は天運にまかせて、
をしまずいとはず、
身をば浮雲になずらへて、
たのまずまだしとせず。

Subete kayō no koto,
tanoshiku tomeru hito ni taishite iu ni wa arazu.

Tada waga mi hitotsu ni torite,
mukashi to ima to o takuraburu bakari nari.

Ōkata yo o nogare,
mi o suteteshi yori,
urami mo naku osore mo nashi.

Inochi wa ten'un ni makasete,
oshimazu itowazu,
mi o ba ukigumo ni nazuraete,
tanomazu madashi to sezu.

I take singular joy in resting my head upon the pillow.

To gaze upon beauty,
That's contentment.

一期のたのしみは、
うたゝねの枕の上にきはまり、
生涯の望は、
をりをりの美景にのこれり。

Ichigo no tanoshimi wa,
utatane no makura no ue ni kiwamari,
shōgai no nozomi wa,
oriori no bikei ni nokoreri.

Transcendence

12
The Life of Solitude

The three realms of existence,
　　—past, present, and future—
Unite in my heart.

Oxen and horses, palaces and mansions:
　　If the heart is not at ease,
　　These worldly treasures bring no pleasure.

I love my lonely dwelling,
This simple, one-room hut.

Sometimes, when I visit the capital,
I feel shame for looking like a beggar.

閑居の氣味

それ三界は、たゞ心一つなり。

心もし安からずは、
牛馬七珍もよしなく、
宮殿樓閣も望なし。

今さびしきすまひ、
ひとまの庵、
みづからこれを愛す。

おのづから都に出でゝは、
乞食となれることをはづといへども、

Kankyo no kimi

Sore sangai wa, tada kokoro hitotsu nari.

Kokoro moshi yasukarazu wa,
gyūba shicchin mo yoshinaku,
kyūden rōkaku mo nozomi nashi.

Ima sabishiki sumai,
hitoma no iori,
mizukara kore o aisu.

Onozukara miyako ni idete wa,
kojiki to nareru koto o hazu to iedomo,

But when I return home,
I feel only pity for those who remain attached to the world.

If you question my sincerity,
I respond with a comparison to fish and birds:
     One cannot doubt a fish's love for the water without experiencing water like a fish does.
     One cannot doubt a bird's love of the forest without seeing the forest through a bird's eyes.

The same goes for the life of solitude:
How could one love it like I do without experiencing it for oneself?

かへりてこゝに居る時は、
他の俗塵に着することをあはれぶ。

もし人このいへることをうたがはゞ、
魚と鳥との分野を見よ。

魚は水に飽かず、
魚にあらざればその心をいかでか知らむ。

鳥は林をねがふ、
鳥にあらざればその心をしらず。

閑居の氣味もまたかくの如し。

住まずしてたれかさとらむ。

kaerite koko ni iru toki wa,
hoka no zokujin ni chakusuru koto o awarebu.

Moshi hito kono ieru koto o utagawaba,
sakana to tori to no bun'ya o miyo.

Sakana wa mizu ni akazu,
sakana ni arazareba sono kokoro o ikade ka shiramu.

Tori wa hayashi o negau,
tori ni arazareba sono kokoro o shirazu.

Kankyo no kimi mo mata kaku no gotoshi.

Sumazu shite tareka satoramu.

13
The Waning Moon

The moon of my life is waning,
Setting gently behind the hills.

At any time now,
I may descend into the River of Eternity.[33]

What good are these musings?

The Buddha taught non-attachment,
And yet, the way I love my grass hut,
That itself is attachment.

I shall waste no more time,
Writing of useless things.

一期の月影かたぶきて

そもそも一期の月影かたぶきて
餘算山のはに近し。

忽に三途のやみにむかはむ時、
何のわざをかかこたむとする。

佛の人を教へ給ふおもむきは、
ことにふれて執心なかれとなり。

今草の庵を愛するもとがとす、
閑寂に着するもさはりなるべし。

いかゞ用なきたのしみをのべて、
むなしくあたら時を過さむ。

Ichigo no tsukikage katabukite

*Somosomo ichigo no tsukikage katabukite
yosan yama no ha ni chikashi.*

*Niwaka ni Sanzu no yami ni mukawamu toki,
nan no waza o ka kakotamu to suru.*

*Hotoke no hito o oshietamau omomuki wa,
koto ni furete shūshin nakare to nari.*

*Ima kusa no iori o aisuru mo toga to su,
kanjyaku ni chakusuru mo sawari narubeshi.*

*Ikaga yō naki tanoshimi o nobete,
munashiku atara toki o sugosamu.*

14
The Quiet of Dawn

In the quiet of dawn, I reflect,
And ask myself:
    You left the world,
    To live in the woods,
    To quiet your mind,
    And follow the Way.

    Although you resemble a monk,
    Your heart is soaked in sin.

    You modeled your home on the hermitage of
    Vimalakīrti.[34]

    Your practice is not as profound as Cūḍapanthaka.[35]

しづかなる曉

しづかなる曉、
このことわりを思ひつゞけて、
みづから心に問ひていはく、
世をのがれて山林にまじはるは、
心をさめて道を行はむがためなり。

然るを汝が姿はひじりに似て、
心はにごりにしめり。

すみかは則ち淨名居士のあとを
けがせりといへども、
たもつ所は、
わづかに周利槃特が行にだも及ばず。

Shizuka naru akatsuki

Shizuka naru akatsuki,
kono kotowari o omoitsuzukete,
mizukara kokoro ni toite iwaku,
yo o nogarete sanrin ni majiwaru wa,
kokoro o osamete michi o okonawamu ga tame nari.

Shikaru o nanji ga sugata wa hijiri ni nite,
kokoro wa nigori ni shimeri.

Sumika wa sunawachi Jyōmyōkoji no ato o
kegaseri to iedomo,
tamotsu tokoro wa,
wazukani Shurihandoku ga gyō ni da mo oyobazu.

Does your wretched karma trouble you?

Has not your critical mind only served to drive you mad?

To these rhetorical questions,
There are no true answers.

So I respond by chanting unbidden prayers to Amida.[36]

And then silence.

Written by the priest Ren'in,
In a hut near Toyama.[37]
On about the last day of the third month,
Second year of the Kenryaku era.*

---

*1213

もしこれ貧賤の報のみづからなやますか、
はた亦妄心のいたりてくるはせるか。

その時こゝろ更に答ふることなし。

たゝ、かたはらに舌根をやとひて不請の念佛、
両三遍を申してやみぬ。

時に建暦の二とせ、
彌生の晦日比、

桑門蓮胤、
外山の庵にしてこれをしるす。

Moshi kore hinsen no mukui no mizukara nayamasu ka,
hata mata mōshin no itarite kuruwaseru ka.

Sono toki kokoro sara ni kotauru koto nashi.

Tata katawara ni zekkon o yatoite fushō no nenbutsu,
ryō sanben o moshite yaminu.

Toki ni Kenryaku no ni to se,
Yayoi no tsugomori koro,

Sōmon Ren'in,
Toyama no iori ni shite kore o shirusu.

Endnotes

1. Like most premodern authors, Chōmei never refers to the capital by name. Instead, he uses the common noun *miyako*, which simply means "the capital." The name Heian-kyō 平安京, which is common in popular writing, was almost never used, not even during the Heian period (794–1180s). It appears in an eighth-century poem composed around the time of the city's establishment and then only sporadically thereafter, almost always as a poetic sobriquet. Heian-kyō became popular during the modern era when officials and public intellectuals sought to romanticize Japan's distant past.

2. During the late twelfth century, the warrior-aristocrat Taira no Kiyomori 平清盛 (1118–1181) had seized control over the court and the primary organs of government. In 1180, he attempted to move the capital to his family's base of power near the Inland Sea. Although Chōmei never names the new city in *Hōjōki*, it appears in historical sources as Fukuhara-kyō 福原京. Fukuhara-kyō's location corresponds closely to modern Kobe. The unfinished site was abandoned six months later, after which the capital returned to the Kyoto basin.

3. In fact, the capital was established earlier, in 794, during the reign of Emperor Kanmu 桓武 (r. 781–806). Chōmei's misunderstanding can be explained by a political row that took place during Saga's reign in which, among other things, there was a debate over whether to move the capital or not.

4. This passage is referring to the dismantling and recycling of building materials. This practice was so common during the premodern era that the authors of historical records tended to make special mention of the rare cases when a structure was built entirely of new materials.

5. Members of the court were generally expected to travel in ox-driven carriages (*gissha* 牛車). By referring to the rising popularity of horses, Chōmei is signaling a transition to more provincial ways and maybe even a preference for the modes indicative of warriors.

6. The Taira house held sway in the archipelago's east, particularly along the Inland Sea.

7. The Maro Palace (Ki no Maro-dono 木の丸殿) is celebrated in literature as a provincial lodge used by the seventh-century female emperor who reigned twice, first as Emperor Kōgyoku 皇極 (r. 642–645) and again as Emperor Saimei 斉明 (r. 655–661). See, for example, book 8 of *Heike monogatari* 平家物語 (*The Tale of the Heike*).

8. Strict codes governing status-specific comportment and consumption informed Chōmei's sense of foreboding. The breakdown of those codes marked a fundamental erosion of the social fabric.

9. The Yōwa era began in the late summer of 1181 and lasted only 10 months. Changing era names was a common practice in times of strife because it was meant to signal (or perhaps elicit) renewal. The famine of Yōwa is well documented and is thought to have been exacerbated by the war between the warrior houses of Taira and Minamoto.

10. Commoners in the premodern capital tended to leave their dead in or near rivers. Only the rich engaged in cremation or burial.

11. Ninnaji was (and remains) an esoteric Shingon temple in Kyoto's northwest. The "holy mark" to which Chōmei refers is the first letter of the Sanskrit orthography (*a* अ), which in Shingon teaching is said to encompass the universe.

12. The boundaries of the capital described here correspond to the original city's eastern half, or Sakyō 左京, meaning "the right capital." The western half, or Ukyō 右京, had never developed as planned and, by the twelfth century, had become cultivated land or scrub. For details, see Matthew Stavros, *Kyoto: An Urban History of Japan's Premodern Capital* (University of Hawai'i Press, 2014), pp. 89–93.

13. Shirakawa was located about half a mile (one kilometer) east of the capital at a site parallel with the Imperial Palace. It developed rapidly after 1075 when Emperor Shirakawa 白河 (1053–1129) started building a massive temple-palace complex based around the temple of Hosshōji 法勝寺. After the emperor's retirement in 1087, the eponymous temple-palace complex became his residential headquarters and the de facto center of government for the next three decades. See Stavros, *Kyoto*, pp. 69–72.

14. It was common to refer to the capital's "seven mouths" 七口, which marked the passages to the seven major highways leading to the provinces. Precisely where these "mouths" were and to which highways they were connected is not known.

15. Emperor Sūtoku reigned from 1123 to 1142.

16. Historical sources confirm that a massive earthquake shook Kyoto on the ninth day of the seventh month, 1185. That was the second year of the Genryaku era. However, because the era name was changed to Bunji 文治 only a month later, most scholars refer to the event as the Great Bunji Earthquake.

17. This is a reference to a tsunami that hit Japan in that year, which is corroborated by other historical sources.

18. The temple of Tōdaiji 東大寺 in Nara was built in the early eighth century by Emperor Shōmu 聖武 (701–756) to protect the nation. Its great bronze Buddha represents the celestial Buddha Vairocana. The structure in which it is housed is the largest wooden building in the world. Both the statue and the building are registered UNESCO World Heritage properties.

19. Ōhara is an area northeast of the capital, famous for the temple of Sanzen'in 三千院.

20. *Hōjō* 方丈 is an architectural term representing an area of one square *jō* 丈, or about 3.03 m². It is the same word used to signify a monk's quarters, primarily at Zen temples.

21. Hino is an area southeast of modern Kyoto, celebrated as the home of the temple of Hōkaiji 法界寺. The hills behind the temple are called Toyama 外山, a name that appears further along in the text and in the colophon.

22. Amida (Sk. Amitābha) is a celestial Buddha and central figure of Mahayana Buddhism. They were, and continue to be, widely revered in Japan and China as the principal Buddha in Pure Land Buddhism. Amida is thought to escort the faithful to the Pure Land at death.

23. Fugen (Sk. Samantabhadra) is a bodhisattva in Mahayana Buddhism associated with ascetic practice and meditation. Together with Gautama Buddha and his fellow bodhisattva Mañjuśrī, he forms the Shakyamuni trinity. Fudō (Sk. Acala) is a protector deity, particularly

revered in Japan's Shingon tradition, where he is known as Fudō Myō-ō 不動明王.

24. *Ōjōyōshū* 往生要集 (*Essentials of Birth in the Pure Land*) was an influential Buddhist text composed in 985 by the monk Genshin 源信 (942–1017). It is widely believed to have influenced later Pure Land teachers such as Hōnen 法然 (1133–1212) and Shinran 親鸞 (1173–1263). Genshin was a scholar of the Tendai school who, having trained in both esoteric and exoteric teachings, wrote several treatises pertaining to Pure Land thought from a Tendai perspective. He is also known as Eshin Sōzu 恵心僧都.

25. Purple clouds are associated with the Western Pure Land where Amida Buddha resides.

26. Chōmei is making a literary reference to a poem by Manshami (also known as Sami Mansei 沙弥満誓) in the *Man'yōshū* 万葉集 (*Anthology of Ten Thousand Leaves*), the oldest extant collection of Japanese *waka* poetry, compiled in the eighth century. Okanoya is a riverside town near Uji, south of modern Kyoto.

27. The Xunyang River is a tributary of the Yangtze in China. As explained in the translation of *Hōjōki* by Moriguchi and Jenkins, Chōmei is referring to a poem by the celebrated Tang poet Bai Juyi 白居易 (772–846). Minamoto no Tsunenobu 源経信 (1016–1097) was a Japanese nobleman and celebrated *waka* poet during the Heian period. One of his poems is included in the *Ogura Hyakunin Isshu* 小倉百人一首 (*Poems from One Hundred Poets, Ogura Edition*), where he is called Dainagon Tsunenobu 大納言経信.

28. "Song of Autumn Breezes" is a score written for Japanese zither (*koto*). "Flowing Water" is an advanced piece for the lute (*biwa*).

29. These sites are *makura-kotoba* 枕詞, figures of speech used in Japanese *waka* poetry where epithets are used in association with certain words.

30. The temple of Ishiyama-dera 石山寺 is located in Shiga Prefecture, near the southern end of Lake Biwa. It is famous for having served as a retreat to Murasaki Shikibu 紫式部, the author of *Genji monogatari* 源氏物語 (*The Tale of Genji*).

31. Makinoshima is in present-day Uji.

32. The text refers to a metaphysical term from Sanskrit (Jp. *gokumi*, Sk. *paramāṇu*) that signifies the smallest possible division of matter, similar to the atom. Chōmei is likely alluding to a Buddhist sutra that made him mindful of human transience and fragility. Despite that fragility, he does not shy away from labor.

33. The Sanzu River, or River of Three Crossings, is a mythological river in Japanese Buddhism. It is similar to the Hindu concept of the Vaitarna and Greek concept of the Styx.

34. Vimalakīrti is the central figure in the Vimalakīrti Sutra. He is depicted as the ideal Mahayana Buddhist lay practitioner and a contemporary of the historical Buddha.

35. Chōmei was probably being ironic. Cūḍapanthaka, a legendary disciple of the Buddha, is known for being dim-witted. He was reportedly unable to understand dharma teachings.

36. This cryptic phrase has received much attention by scholars over the years. For details, see Thomas B. Hare, "Reading Kamo no Chōmei," *Harvard Journal of Asiatic Studies*, vol. 49, No. 1. (Jun., 1989), pp. 173–228.

37. Chōmei may have used the name Ren'in to signify that he had taken Buddhist vows and thus assumed a new identity.

To Access Audio Recordings:

1. Check to be sure you have an Internet connection.
2. Type the URL below into your web browser.

https://www.tuttlepublishing.com/hojoki

For support, you can email us at info@tuttlepublishing.com.

"Books to Span the East and West"

Tuttle Publishing was founded in 1832 in the small New England town of Rutland, Vermont [USA]. Our core values remain as strong today as they were then—to publish best-in-class books which bring people together one page at a time. In 1948, we established a publishing outpost in Japan—and Tuttle is now a leader in publishing English-language books about the arts, languages and cultures of Asia. The world has become a much smaller place today and Asia's economic and cultural influence has grown. Yet the need for meaningful dialogue and information about this diverse region has never been greater. Over the past seven decades, Tuttle has published thousands of books on subjects ranging from martial arts and paper crafts to language learning and literature—and our talented authors, illustrators, designers and photographers have won many prestigious awards. We welcome you to explore the wealth of information available on Asia at www.tuttlepublishing.com.

Published by Tuttle Publishing, an imprint of Periplus Editions (HK) Ltd.

www.tuttlepublishing.com

Copyright © 2024 Matthew Stavros

All photographs and maps are by the author.

Library of Congress Catalog-in-Publication Data in progress

ISBN 978-4-8053-1800-3

First edition
27 26 25 24   5 4 3 2 1   2312CM

Printed in China

TUTTLE PUBLISHING® is a registered trademark of Tuttle Publishing, a division of Periplus Editions (HK) Ltd.

Distributed by:

North America, Latin America & Europe
Tuttle Publishing
364 Innovation Drive
North Clarendon
VT 05759 9436, USA
Tel: 1(802) 773 8930
Fax: 1(802) 773 6993
info@tuttlepublishing.com
www.tuttlepublishing.com

Japan
Tuttle Publishing
Yaekari Building, 3rd Floor
5-4-12 Osaki Shinagawa-ku
Tokyo 141 0032 Japan
Tel: 81 (3) 5437 0171
Fax: 81 (3) 5437 0755
sales@tuttle.co.jp
www.tuttle.co.jp

Asia Pacific
Berkeley Books Pte Ltd
3 Kallang Sector #04-01
Singapore 349278
Tel: (65) 6741-2178
Fax: (65) 6741-2179
inquiries@periplus.com.sg
www.tuttlepublishing.com